A FOOL'S RETURN

Also by William de Lange:

A Fool's Journey

Musashi: Fact & Fiction
Famous Samurai, I, II, III
The Real Musashi, I, II, III
Miyamoto Musashi: A Life in Arms
A History of Japanese Journalism
A Dictionary of Japanese Onomatopoeia
A Dictionary of Japanese Proverbs
A Dictionary of Japanese Idioms
Japanese Scrolls
Pars Japonica
Iaido

A Fool's Return

Walking Japan's Coastal Route in Search of Beauty

William de Lange

Toyo Press

For more on books by William de Lange visit:
www.williamdelange.com

First edition, 2020

Published by TOYO Press
Visit us at: **www.toyopress.com**

ISBN 978-94-92722-249

For Kyōko, Teppei, and Minako

I never want to grow up,
but I always want to keep on growing.
— Arthur C. Clark

Contents

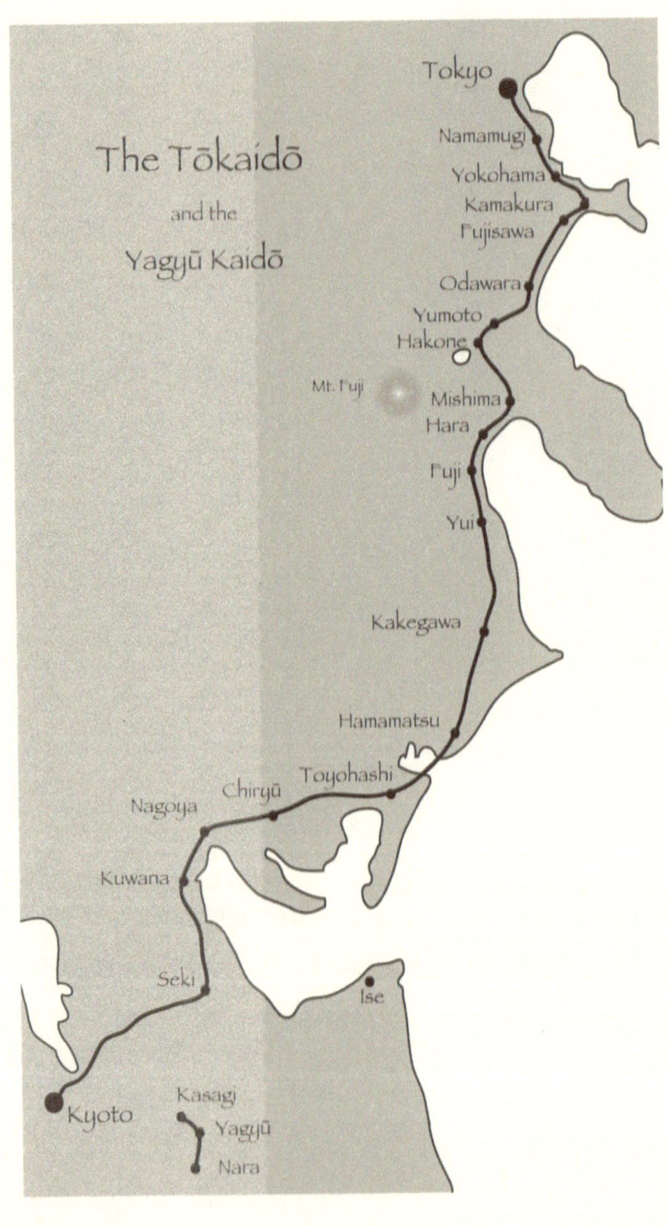

The Tōkaidō
and the
Yagyū Kaidō
Tokyo
Namamugi
Yokohama
Kamakura
Fujisawa
Odawara
Yumoto
Hakone
Mt. Fuji
Mishima
Hara
Fuji
Yui
Kakegawa
Hamamatsu
Toyohashi
Chiryū
Nagoya
Kuwana
Seki
Ise
Kyoto
Kasagi
Yagyū
Nara

Ticket

It was the summer of 1989, a year before the outbreak of the
First Gulf War. I had bought myself an open-ended return
ticket to Japan with Iraqi Airways, the cheapest on offer. At
its hub of Baghdad airport, big women in wide black *aba*
shepherded passengers around as if they were cattle. The
airport had only been completed seven years earlier. It had
been a Franco-Iraqi cooperation, modeled after Charles de
Gaulle International Airport, though none of the computers
or screens at the terminals worked. In some downstairs
corridor that functioned as a transit area, we were served tea
and coffee from a small trolley, poured from rugged steel
canisters that looked like they had come straight off the back
of a Land Rover.

Flying back, half a year later, I would be just in time to
miss the hostage crisis in the run-up to the Gulf War. The
Iraqis had captured more than eight hundred foreigners in
Iraq and Kuwait and been forced to serve as human shields

to protect strategic sites throughout Iraq from Coalition bombers. I can still remember watching the news, only a few weeks before I entered Leiden University to take up my Japanese studies. There, on the screen, was Saddam Hussein, immaculately dressed in white, sitting in a chair, with the usual smug grin on his face, ruffling the hair of a terrified small boy who refused to sit on his lap. Though the boy was soon released, his father would be held captive until Christmas. Had I returned home only a few months later, I too might have been among those hostages, stuck in Iraq for three terrifying months.

I had earned my ticket painting houses for a student friend's father who owned a lot of properties in Groningen. It being a university town, most of them housed students. I noticed then how none would ever ask you if you needed a refreshment. They could be gathered in the kitchen, discussing grave social issues, the windows wide open, and not care to even say hello as I was painting their window sills. This in sharp contrast with the elderly ladies who occupied the houses my old friend and I had painted for the slum landlord when I was younger. They, on the other hand, couldn't wait to invite you in for a cup of coffee or tea and provide some diversion to their otherwise lackluster days. To the students, I was just a blue-collar laborer, part of a different class of society—not to be mingled with. And this even though I too was now a student, studying English and living in one of the houses I had painted.

It was also the year of the Tiananmen Square Massacre. Not owning a television—I still don't—I got most of my news from the BBC World Service. It was something I did as part of my English studies, although by then my Japanese 'hobby' had already taken over. Every day I spent hours on my kanji, the thousands of Chinese characters that make up part of the complex Japanese writing system. Over the previous weeks I had been following developments closely, the student's initial protests, their building of their crudely crafted statue of liberty, their heroic but naive attempts at negotiating with a unyielding regime, and finally the last desperate attempts by the moderate Zhao Ziyang to persuade them to leave the square and return to their dormitories. Though written in the simplified script introduced in the 1950s, I could already read many of the characters on their banners; they spoke of human rights, freedom of expression, democracy.

Then came the dreadful day of the crackdown. I distinctly remember sitting in my kitchen listening to the radio as an audibly shaken BBC reporter called through the latest news from Beijing. At first, it was sketchy—troops being moved in, occasional bursts of rifle fire, tanks on the streets. But within hours it became clear that the standoff had escalated into something far more sinister: cyclists had been crushed by tanks, pedestrians mowed down by machine gunfire. Hundreds, possibly thousands of innocent and defenseless citizens were killed in Beijing on that summer evening in

1989, their only crime a wish for a better life. Many others were imprisoned, forcefully exchanging a promising future for a life of persecution and long spells in prison. For a young student with a serious interest in Asia, it came as a shock. It felt as if, with their dream, my own aspirations had also been diminished—a stark reminder that the most fervent hopes could be cruelly crushed by cynical forces indifferent to an individual's personal happiness.

The first real glimpse I got of Asia was when the Iraqi Airways Boeing 747 slowly descended towards Bangkok airport, the second and last stop en route to Japan. What at first had seemed a soft-green checkered blanket gradually changed into a dreamlike landscape. From the window I first saw endless paddy fields, then I began to make out more details: a few scattered houses on stilts, then a few cars and a lone cyclist on a narrow dirt road, and finally, here and there, groups of tiny figures amid the paddies, their wide straw hats tilting in unison as they bucked to plant the new rice crop.

Five hours later we were flying over a glittering Sea of Japan. High above, cotton-like clouds shimmered in a bright blue sky. It was an image that would stay with me forever, that first impression—not so much any physical object, but that bright, white light; as if I were entering a different realm, a magical world beyond the clouds.

Leaving Tokyo

It was now 1219, thirty years after I had first set foot in Japan. This time I was going to walk the Tōkaidō. Two years earlier, I had walked the Nakasendō, the old high road from Kyoto to Edo through the Japanese Alps. Like the Nakasendō, the Tōkaido connects the present and former capital, except that the Tōkaidō largely follows Japan's Pacific coastline. This time I would be walking in the opposite direction; I would set out from Tokyo.

I had always wanted to simply walk out of Tokyo, not so much to leave it behind me—I find it endlessly fascinating—but simply to experience its vastness. In my time as a student, I had extensively traveled it by bus, underground and overground railway, but it had never given me a true sense of its dimensions. Even the bus had served to compress its size, make it more digestible, less overwhelming. I wanted to feel the distances, feel them in my bones and muscles, like the medieval Japanese traveler had done.

Already back then Edo, as it was still called, was one of the world's largest metropolises, home to more than a million Edoites. Today the larger Tokyo region is home to more than thirty-nine million Tokyoites, the combined population of greater New York and greater Los Angeles in an area just one-tenth the size.

This trip was going to be even more foolhardy than the one along the Nakasendō. Now I was determined to find some beauty among the Tōkaidō, most of which now runs through some of Japan's most heavily industrialized regions. I knew it would be a tall order. Many times before, I had passed this stretch of Japan's Pacific coastline, whizzing along on the fabled Shinkansen, always grateful how the train's breathtaking speed helped to gloss over all the ugliness through which it sped. Not once had I spotted a picturesque bay, an old village, or even a stretch of dirt track. Only majestic mount Fuji still reared its magnificent dome in the background as it had done since time immemorial, though now increasingly obscured by modern-day smog. Yet I knew that, somewhere along the route, bits of old Japan remained, along the Hakone Pass at the foot of the Izu Peninsula, and on the last stretch, through the Suzuka Mountains. To find them one had to leave the beaten track, especially the straight and unbending tracks of the Shinkansen.

Of course I had to start my journey at Nihonbashi, the ancient bridge at a stone's throw east of Edo castle. It was the place where the country's main traffic arteries—the Tōkaidō, the Nakasendō, the Nikkō Kaidō, the Ōshū Kaidō, and the Kōshū Kaidō—converged. Even today Nihonbashi is the point from which all highroad distances to the capital are measured.

In those days the bridge was a beautifully curved wooden structure, as immortalized in Hiroshige's instantly recognizable wood prints. A hundred thousand people are said to have daily made their way across the wide bridge, the pitter-patter of their two hundred thousand geta ringing out across the bustling banks of the Nihonbashi River, which at that time was the location of Edo's fish market, the forerunner of today's Tsukiji.

Today, little reminds the passerby of the rich history of the place. Like most of Tokyo's waterways, the river's murky waters now course through a wide duct of concrete, lending it the look of a giant sewage. Overhead looms the multi-lane Shuto Expressway, its massive pylons rudely plodding the course of the river, robbing it of the rays of sunshine that would cast the whole affair in at least a more pleasant light.

The bridge itself is a far cry from the original. An early nineteenth-century creation of stones on a cast-iron structure with stylized lions guarding both ends, it does lend the place its much needed historical touch, partly because it still bears the scars of the massive Allied air raids—which killed more Japanese than the atomic bomb on Nagasaki, the majority women, elderly and children.

As I began to follow the Tōkaidō southward, there seemed no end to the high-rise buildings. At each bend of the road, new towering vistas loomed up in the distance, like in a cheap flight simulator, uniform and faceless, as if they sprang up from nowhere. As usual, there seemed no rhyme or reason to the layout. I cynically reflected it was rather a good thing, really, that so much of Japan was mountainous and practically uninhabitable on such an intense scale. At least those areas would be spared. By the time the mountains would have eroded into pleasant hills, Japan's town planners might just about have got their act together.

Left of me the long snake of a Shinkansen cut its way through the suburban undergrowth, taking just under two and a half hours over what would take me the better part of two weeks.

As I approached Shinagawa I kept running into Western couples, old-age pensioners mostly—pot-bellied men in shorts, clutching hands with wives who brandished handbags with the other as if it were a weapon. They were probably castaways from one of the vast cruise ships that dock at one of the nearby terminals on a daily basis.

At Shinagawa station, the Tōkaidō thankfully parted with the Daiichi Keihin Expressway. Here the old highroad assumed something resembling the scale it must have had during the Edo period. After a mile, I passed the Shinagawa-*dera*, the temple where my old Buddhist friend, Vincent, had been training in the early nineties and caught out a fellow novice wearing a fake Rolex. It had also been the place where he had walked on burning coals during the temple's annual Shukuba *matsuri*, a festival celebrating Shinagawa's history as the first rest stop along the Tōkaidō. It was now May and the place lay bare. Only a scorched concrete slab marked the place where the blistering festival had taken place on that warm September evening.

Student

The dormitory of the Japanese Ministry of Education in Tokyo's Seijō ward had been a melting pot of cultures. I got to know Yonas from Ethiopia, who showed me pictures of home on his new Japanese laptop, a small village set amid green pastures in mountainous countryside.

I got to know Gero, a German who was doing research for his master's at Tōdai University. He had once considered taking up music in earnest but had decided he didn't have it in him. He still played the piano brilliantly, though, engendering in me a lifelong love of Scriabin. He also played the violin, using its case as a doorstop to get some fresh air into his cramped dormitory room.

Then there was the French guy of Chinese descent whose name I have now forgotten, but who said he belonged to a long line of practitioners of the Shaoling school of martial arts. On weekends he went bare-hand rock climbing in the Japanese Alps with like-minded sporty types. I was suffering from a slight stomach ulcer at the time, and he told me to stand flat against the wall. Over the next few minutes, he pilloried my abdomen with a series of targeted blows with both his index fingers. The pain at first was excruciating, but when he stopped it transmorphed into a warm, soothing glow that spread throughout my bowels and lasted for hours.

I also got to know Anthony, who studied at Jōchi University and was a member of the U.K. kendō team. I stayed with him and his parents in England once. His father, a big whig at what was then still the Hong Kong Shanghai Bank, took us to his favorite local pub for a pint of real ale and we talked about what we intended to do once we had completed our Japanese studies. I told him of my writing aspirations. He had frowned and studiously examined the bottom of his empty pint glass and said, 'But what are you going to do at the end of the day, William?' Anthony at the time had still wanted to become a journalist. He ended up doing a stint for the GCHQ, the British signals intelligence agency. The last thing I heard was that he had done a speed course in law and was now working for a legal firm in Japan, though he still seemed to be on the UK kendō team.

And I met Nadja. She wasn't in my dorm but in that of Waseda University. We were placed in the second class during the second semester. In fact, she had moved up one grade because of her brilliance in language. One day we were walking back along Waseda Dōri towards Takada no

Baba station when she asked me if I had any plans for the weekend. Flustered, I said I was going to a fencing demonstration with Anthony. I regretted it the moment I said it: why do something with a bloke if you can spend time with a beautiful girl? The demonstration was disappointing, and I spent a bored weekend thinking about Nadja.

The next weekend, I took her swimming at Katsura, the hometown of Taeko-*san*, my foster mother. There, in a small cove away from the village, with the Pacific swell lapping at our feet, we kissed for the first time.

At the dorm, we had watched Giuseppe Tornatore's wonderfully nostalgic Cinema Paradiso. I immediately bought the film music by Ennio Morricone, and for the next few months, it became the sound track to one of my best years in Japan: breakfasts at Denny's with Nadja, fencing practice with my old teacher, Satake *sensei*, at the local police station, and warm evenings with student friends on the town.

During our last weeks in Japan, when our Japanese language classes had finished, Nadja and I traveled up the coast towards the Oshika Peninsula, just north of Sendai. Most of the small fishing communities we visited en route would be wiped away in the tsunami that hit the region in 2011. At less than seventy-five kilometers, the Oshika Peninsula was closest to the earthquake's epicenter. In its wake, more than a thousand dead bodies washed ashore on a coast that had shifted by more than five meters and sunk by more than a meter. It was the worst disaster to strike Japan since the Second World War, claiming more than twenty thousand lives and displacing some three hundred thousand men, women and children. Whole villages were swept from the face of the earth.

At the tip of the peninsula, at the small fishing port of Ayukawahama, we stayed in a beautiful *ryōkan*. The breakfast they served was a feast. Small baskets with artistically fried *tempura*; bowls with delicate *miso* soup. The red *sashimi*, placed around a large lacquered plate like the petals of an exotic flower, looked like dark tuna, but tasted more like lean beef. When the maids collected the trays I asked them what it was. It was minke whale, just landed by the port's one small whaling vessel. Glowing with pride, they asked us whether we had enjoyed it.

As we left, we saw the source of our breakfast, hauled ashore and surgically cut into pieces by a team of fishermen clad in plastic aprons and white boots.

I had mixed feelings about my 'crime.' I felt terribly sad for this beautiful animal, harpooned and left to bleed to death in its useless struggle to extricate itself. At the same time I realized that for centuries whaling had been Ayukawahama's lifeline: without it, this small fishing community too would be corroded by the ever-spreading cancer of modernity.

Rebellion

A few miles farther down the Tōkaidō, I passed the former Suzugamori execution grounds. Together with Kotsujappara along the Nikkō highroad at Edo's northern entrance, and Oowada, on the northern bank of the Asakawa River along the Kōshū highroad at Edo's western entrance, it was the a place where criminals were executed and their severed heads put on display, reminding incoming travelers to behave or face the consequences. Especially during the early years of the Edo period, the Tokugawa authorities intended these strategically situated grounds as a deterrent against *rōnin*, *samurai* who had lost their master following Japan's pacification after centuries of civil war.

The first to be put to death at Suzugamori was Marobashi Chūya, a fencing instructor from Yamagata. Chūya's father had died fighting the Tokugawa during the siege of Osaka castle in 1615. To revenge his father, Chūya became one of the ringleaders in the Keian Rebellion, so named after the

Keian era (1646–52). It was in the spring of the era's penultimate year that, shortly after the demise of Shōgun Tokugawa Iemitsu, Chūya and a number of other disgruntled *rōnin* sought to topple the Tokugawa Bakufu. Ever since Iemitsu's grandfather, Ieyasu, had unified the country in the Battle of Sekigahara and the Siege of Osaka castle, the Bakufu had come down hard on those who had opposed them. Iemitsu, in particular, had alienated a lot of *samurai* by confiscating their and their lords' possessions. As a result, the number of *rōnin* during his reign had exploded. Some turned to farming or trading to support themselves, others to crime. Others yet sought to pursue a career abroad. They convened on Japan's major port towns, hoping to board a ship and follow in the footsteps of men like Yamada Nagamasa, who had become an influential governor in the Atutthaya Kingdom on the Malay Peninsula. But even this path was cut off when, in 1639, the Bakufu closed the country's borders to keep out foreign missionaries. It left Japan's ports awash with *rōnin* seething with resentment at their unjust treatment.

In a move reminiscent of Guy Fawkes' Gunpowder Plot, Chūya and his fellow conspirators intended to capture Edo castle using barrels of gunpowder. But the plot was uncovered when Chūya fell ill and in his feverish delirium divulged sensitive information. Word soon reached the authorities, who immediately moved to arrest him. His fellow conspirators, realizing their game was up, committed ritual suicide.

An investigation was launched into the reasons behind the rebellion, and wisely, the authorities decided to steer away from any widespread persecution. Instead, they chose to ease the *rōnin*'s path back into employment. Yet Marobashi Chūya and the families of the conspirators were put to death, mostly after long hours of torture.

Between its inception in 1561 and its closure in 1861, some two hundred thousand people were executed at Suzugamori. Most were beheaded, but some were drowned in the then still nearby waters of Edo Bay. Like other execution grounds, it was also a place where newly forged swords were tested by stacking the remaining torsos into piles and cutting through them in one blow. Antique swords that once passed this test still carry under their hilts the engravings to prove it—'three-torso cut,' 'four-torso cut,' or even 'five-torso cut.'

Namamugi

Having seen nineteenth-century photos of Japanese execution grounds, I was glad I wasn't traveling during Japan's feudal era, when one could get killed just by rubbing a *samurai* the wrong way. There were plenty examples of that, even of foreigners who had gotten on the wrong side of a *samurai*. Especially during the closing days of the Bakufu, when ill-informed foreigners began to travel outside the confines of the foreign settlement in Yokohama, there was a spate of such incidents.

One such incident had occurred at the hamlet of Namamugi, then halfway between Edo and Yokohama. Some three hours after I had left the former site of the Suzugamori execution grounds behind me, I passed through Namamugi, which today has been swallowed up by Tokyo's Tsurumi ward. I had always wanted to visit Namamugi, though, except for a commemorative plaque, there was little of interest to see in this otherwise nondescript Tokyo suburb.

Judging by the peaceful domesticity of the place, few would imagine it had once been the scene of a dreadful killing.

The Namamugi Incident, as it has come to be known in Japan and abroad, seems to sum up perfectly the clash of cultures that attended Japan's involuntary opening up to the West. Even today, one and a half centuries after it happened, the incident holds a particular spell among the Japanese. Not a year goes by without some film or TV documentary delving into this particular episode from the closing days of Japan's feudal era. Japan's struggle to adjust to its new place in the world, its wounded sense of pride; the West's ill-conceived notions of the Orient, its imperialistic sense of superiority—all seemed to come together on that fateful sultry summer day of September 14, 1862, when a Britt named Charles Lennox Richardson came face to face with a *samurai* named Narahara Kizaemon.

Richardson had been on his way back to Europe when he stopped over at Yokohama to spend some of his newly accumulated wealth. He appears to have been glad to get away from China. After some fourteen years in Kanton and Shanghai, he was, in his own words, 'sick of this place.' Japan, by contrast, seemed to the merchant a promising new commercial frontier, 'a country out of which great things will come.' To further explore this fascinating country, he had persuaded three of his newly made expat friends in Yokohama to join him on an excursion on horseback along the ancient Tōkaidō.

They had been on the road for just an hour, when, near the hamlet of Namamugi, they encountered the retinue of Shimazu Saburō (Hisamitsu), father and regent of the young Shimazu Tadayoshi, the *daimyō* of the Satsuma domain on Japan's southern island of Kyushu. Consisting of a total of some seven hundred men, the procession was on its way from Edo to Kyoto, the opposite direction in which Richardson and his friends were traveling.

What followed is described in riveting detail in the diary of Ernest Mason Satow, a British Japanologist who had arrived in Japan only a few days earlier to take up a position as an interpreter at the British Japan Consular Service in Yokohama:

On the 14th September, a most barbarous murder was committed on a Shanghai merchant named Richardson. He, in company with a mrs. Margaret Watson Borradaile of Hongkong, and Woodthorpe Charles Clarke and William Marshall, both of Yokohama, were riding along the highroad between Kanagawa and Kawasaki, when they met with a train of the *daimyō*'s retainers, who bid them stand aside. They passed on at the edge of the road, until they came in sight of a palanquin, occupied by Shimazu Saburō, father of the Prince of Satsuma. They were now ordered to turn back, and as they were wheeling their horses in obedience, were suddenly set upon by several armed men belonging to the train, who hacked at them with their sharp-edged heavy swords. Richardson fell from his horse in a dying state, and the other two men were so severely wounded that they called out to the lady: 'Ride on, we can do nothing for you.' She got safely back to Yokohama and gave the alarm. Everybody in the settlement who possessed a pony and a revolver at once armed himself and galloped off towards the scene of slaughter.

Satow's account was corroborated by the Australian travel writer, Samuel Mossman, who in his book *New Japan: The Land of the Rising Sun* relates that:

On further inquiry of the people in the neighborhood, they said that Mr. Richardson was able to reach a bank by the roadside, where he sat under a tree, close to a small tea shed kept by a woman. Though dreadfully wounded by a gash sixteen inches long, severing his ribs and opening his abdomen, with a severe wound across one hand dividing the fingers, he was able to sit up and ask for *mizu* (water), the only word almost that he knew of the Japanese language.

A pretty damning inditement by Satow and Mossman there. But as usual, the truth was a bit more complicated. Other contemporary records gave a somewhat different account of events. There were, for instance, the depositions of Richardson's companions, Clarke and Marshall. The latter stated that, immediately before Richardson had met his end, 'Clarke said, "Don't go on, we can turn into a side road.' Marshall agreed: 'For God's sake, let us not have a row.' But Richardson ignored them. 'Let me alone,' he replied, 'I have lived in China for fourteen years, I know how to manage these people.' This impression of a typically imperialist English merchant was borne out by Richardson's uncle, who said he didn't blame the Japanese. In his words: 'Charles was incredibly reckless and stubborn,' and 'had to leave England because of his crazy stunts.'

It seems indeed, that the key to Richardson's behavior lies in his experience as a merchant in China. Frederich Wright-Bruce, the British envoy to China, who had known Richardson in Shanghai, remembered him as an 'arrogant adventurer.' Richardson, in the envoy's estimation, was:

> Of a type too often found among our middle class. With the brutal courage of a prizefighter, unimpeded by a single chivalrous instinct. The instincts of these men are developed among the debasing insolence of a life in the East. They acquire a taste for inflicting suffering, by practicing it on people who don't resist.

The envoy had come to this stark conclusion after he had been obliged to punish Richardson after an incident with a

Chinese servant. Richardson had been among a party of four young 'gentlemen,' who had taken offense at the servant warming himself before their fire. They had assaulted him so badly that he had to be hospitalized. Three of them had been fined for the assault, but Richardson more heavily, as he was deemed the main instigator. They also faced deportation if they were caught doing it again.

It wasn't as if Richardson repented his callous act. Writing to his 'dear mama' back home in England, he confessed:

> The truth is, the man was insolent, and I knocked him down. I was the only person to blame for striking the animal; the others had nothing to do with it.

Narahara Kizaemon, by contrast, the Shimazu retainer who cut Richardson down from his horse, seems to have been a conscientious man who had followed the typical *samurai*'s career path. Born in the shadow of Kagoshima castle, Kizaemon was a practitioner of the Yakumaru Shigen school of swordsmanship and an accomplished archer. For a while, he had served Shōgun Tokugawa Yoshinobu but seems to have fallen short of what was expected of him. On his return to Satsuma, he entered the service of Shimazu Saburō, and one of his first assignments was to escort his lord to Edo in the capacity of *tomometsuke*, or 'inspector accompanying a *daimyō*'s procession.' It was on their return that they ran into Richardson and his fellow travelers.

The initial official Japanese standpoint, too, was that Kizaemon had done nothing wrong. It was simply unheard of in Japan, not to 'stand down and sit down' (*geba-geza*) alongside the road whenever one happened to encounter a retinue of one of Japan's two hundred *daimyō* on their annual trip to Edo or back home to their domain. Like any good retainer, Kizaemon had exercised a *samurai*'s prerogative of *kirisute gomen*, the 'authorization to cut and leave' for dead anyone who refused to pay his lord due respect. In their perspective, it had not been Kizaemon, but Richardson who had been at fault by not honoring longstanding Japanese traditions.

There was also the starkly contrasting example of the Dutch-American merchant Eugene Miller van Reed, who had also ran into Hisamitsu's procession and had the courtesy (or at least the common sense) to get off his horse and bow for the *daimyō*. It had not only saved him his life but won him the eternal respect of the Japanese—albeit at the cost of the vilification of the foreign community, who generally felt Westerners were above such stoopings.

Just how much the tension had already been building is clear from communications between Satsuma and the Bakufu authorities in Edo. Even prior to his departure from Satsuma, Saburō's counselors had written to the Bakufu to complain about the 'intolerable behavior of foreigners on the Tōkaidō. In response, the Bakufu had warned leaders of the foreign missions in Yokohama, including the British chargé d'affaires, Edward Neale, for all foreigners to stay away from the Tōkaidō during Saburō's journey.

It was for all the above reasons that the Satsuma authorities felt they had been justified in their actions and stubbornly refused to pay the twenty-five thousand Pounds demanded by the British. They also refused to turn over Kizaemon and the *samurai* who had wounded Clarke.

In this they went against the wishes of the Shōgun, who for the sake of international relationships, had paid the one hundred thousand pounds the English had additionally demanded from the Bakufu, even though it was a staggering third of their annual revenue—just imagine the reverse!

The standoff between Britain and Satsuma continued amid rising tensions, fanned on the one hand by the belligerence of the British, on the other hand by the constant prevarications and procrastinations on the side of the Satsuma authorities.

Legally the Japanese didn't have a leg to stand on. Enjoying extraterritoriality under the Treaty of Amity and Commerce of 1858, foreigners were exempt from prosecution under Japanese law. The treaty, composed of a whole raft of clauses favorable to the United States, curtailed Japanese sovereignty for the first time in its long history. Officially, it had been 'negotiated' by the United States Consul General Townsend Harris. In truth, it had been imposed on the Japanese in the wake of Commander Matthew Calbraith Perry's gunboat diplomacy. The ink on the treaty was hardly dry when other foreign powers imposed similarly self-serving treaties on the Japanese.

The measure of extraterritoriality was ostensibly meant to protect foreigners from the growing anti-foreign sentiments. From today's perspective, it is hard to believe now how they could have failed to see that much of the discontent was caused by these treaties in the first place. What might have set them thinking was that the Japanese referred to them as the 'Unequal Treaties.'

In their imperialist indignation, the British seized three foreign-built ships at anchor in Kagoshima Bay, representing a total worth of two hundred thousand pounds sterling, thus hoping to coerce Satsuma to submit to their demands. It didn't work. Instead, the Japanese fired round shot at the unsuspecting British, who pettily set fire to the ships and proceeded to bombard the town of Kagoshima.

But the Satsuma authorities were prepared. They had evacuated large parts of Kagoshima. As a result, only five of Kagoshima's inhabitants died, while thirteen British sailors lost their lives. The Japanese seemed to have been good marksmen, too, for one of their rounds decapitated both Captain Josling of the British flagship Euryalus, as well as his second-in-command Commander Wilmot.

The material damage was extensive; some five hundred of Kagoshima's wooden dwellings went up in flames. Yet the conflict ended in a victory of sorts for the Japanese. Running low on food and ammunition, the British withdrew without landing any troops. And with twenty killed and fifty-three wounded (against five killed and thirteen wounded on the Japanese side) they also suffered the most casualties.

In the end, Satsuma did pay up the twenty-five thousand Pounds, though they never identified or handed over the men responsible for Richardson's death (though severely wounded by Narahara Kizaemon, the actual coup de grâce was delivered by another Shimazu retainer).

Ironically, the lengthy negotiations resulted in a meeting of minds over Japan's future. They led to close relations between Satsuma and Britain, which became a staunch ally in the Boshin War, the short military conflict between the southern domains and the Tokugawa regime.

Chinatown

That evening, as I checked in at a cheap capsule hotel in downtown Yokoyama, I was pretty exhausted but satisfied: I had walked almost twenty miles on my very first day, breaking my record when I had walked the Nakasendō two years earlier. And I had done what I had set out to do: to walk out of Tokyo. It had entertained few illusions about what I would find along this stretch of the Tōkaidō, so in that sense, I wasn't disappointed. It had reinforced on me the impression of how similar most of Japan's large cities are on their outskirts. Dating no farther back than half a century, Most modern Japanese cities are made up of the same building blocks: high-rise office buildings, low-rise apartment blocks, huge department stores, and lots and lots of semi-prefab housing. Slashing through this urban sprawl, a dense web of overground and above-ground express and super-expressways, rail and Shinkansen tracks, generated a relentless drone that began to grate on my ears like a rusted chainsaw. Only the odd scattered park, temple ground, or shrine set among a small grove, provided a sanctuary of sorts from the constant race that is modern-day transport.

In this respect, the old downtown area of Yokohama was a pleasant exception. Like its equivalents in Sidney, London, New York, and so many other overseas cities, Yokohama's Chinatown has an unmistakable Chinese feel to it, if only because of the typically Chinese shop signs. Together with the red lanterns, glue-on dragon ornaments, and the classic red and gold patterns, they render the place distinctly Chinese, even though most of the buildings behind the gaudy facade are typically modern Japanese post-war structures.

Chūkaigai, as it is called in Japanese, has a history that dates back to the late 1850's, when, in the wake of Commodore Perry's visit, the port of Yokohama was opened to foreign ships after two and a half centuries of self-imposed seclusion. Together with the Westerners came a large number of (mainly) Kanton Chinese, making their living as compradors for the newly established trade routes with Shanghai and Hongkong, or simply in the service of the Westerners who had settled in Yokohama.

Despite the quarter's thoroughly Chinese credentials, I had the greatest difficulty in finding a Peking Duck chop. I had expected to find them in droves, with lines of marinated ducks strung up by their necks behind greasy and steamy shop windows, as one can in London's Chinatown. But none of it here. It seemed the direct confrontation with this somewhat gruesome display of tortured animals didn't appeal to the Japanese culinary sense. They preferred to see immaculate—though equally Chinese—plastic imitations of their favorite dishes on display in pristine settings. Most in vogue was the Chinese dumpling shops, where people were lining up in long rows to have their favorite type of dumplings put in cute paper carrying bags. At length, I found a shop that served Peking duck. It was delicious, though, at three thousand yen, one of the most expensive I would have on my whole trip.

As I sauntered back to my drab capsule hotel on the opposite bank of the Ōoka River, I reflected I would have made it a lot easier—and cheaper—for myself had I instead looked for a *rāmen* shop, if only because this ubiquitous noodle dish originated in Yokohama's China Town, which is aptly home to the world's first *Rāmen* Museum.

I once had an argument with a Ukranian dentist who had worked in Shanghai and was convinced the dish was of Japanese origin: why else all the Japanese *rāmen* restaurants over in China? She was wrong, of course, though her mistake was understandable. Though *rāmen* is of Chinese origin, its precise pedigree is still somewhat disputed.

What is certain is that when the Chinese settled in Yokohama they brought with them the habit of eating *laamian*, a cheap lunch of hand-pulled (*ra*) wheat noodles (*mian*) served in a bowl of steaming chicken broth.

The quick and easy dish soon inspired Tokyo peddlers to

copy and sell them from their small pushcarts on the busy streets of Tokyo's Asakusa and Ueno neighborhoods.

As with all things foreign, the Japanese began to create their own take on this already popular dish, adding typically Japanese condiments like *nori* (dried seaweed), *menma* (pickled bamboo shoots), and *narutomaki* (fish cake). The broth too underwent changes, with ingredients like soy sauce and burnt garlic thrown in to create the rich *umami* flavor of which the Japanese are so fond.

Rāmen's real breakthrough seems to have come in 1910, when the Japanese entrepreneur Ozaki Kenichi, a customs official from the port of Yokohama, opened the Rai-Rai Ken in Tokyo's Asakusa district, the first Japanese-operated establishment to serve *Shina* (China) and Nanking-*soba*, after the then capital of China. It was a huge hit, causing the Japanese *rāmen* critic Ōsaki Hiroshi to baptize the year 1910 the *rāmen gannen*, the 'first year of the *rāmen* era.'

During the American occupation, when food was expensive and in short supply, *Chūka-soba*, as it was now widely called, only grew in popularity, though it did undergo some changes. One was the addition of *chāshū* (*char siu*) Chinese-style marinated pork. Next to the wheat for the noodles, the pork meat could be found on the black markets that sprang up around the country, which in turn drew their goods from the huge quantities of foodstuffs shipped in from America as part of an extensive school lunch program to combat malnourishment among children.

Rāmen's association with Japan's post-war hard times led to a slump in its popularity during the late fifties. Its blue-collar status persevered during the next two decades when it helped feed the vast armies of construction workers who rebuilt Japan and enabled the economic miracle.

But more recently, the *rāmen* shops have experienced a revival, partly as a result of the dish's overseas popularity. Today, along with *sushi*, *rāmen* has become one of Japan's most popular dishes abroad, with high-end *rāmen* restaurants in many foreign capitals. Back home in Japan, there are now some forty thousand *rāmen* shops—a clear sign that the wholesome noodle dish is here to stay. Thankfully, they have also resisted the awful chain-store trend; some eighty percent of Japan's *rāmen* shops are still small businesses, often run by just one person.

Taitō Misaki

It had been in 1994, between my first and second semester while enrolled in the foreign student program at Waseda University, that I worked on the project that had driven me to get a Japanese scholarship: my thesis on Japanese journalism. And I had been lucky enough to do so above the roar of the Pacific. Koyama-*san*, the old friend of the Japanese family with whom I had stayed when I first visited Japan, happened to be sitting on a plot of land near Taitō Misaki, a small headland half-way down the east coast of the Bōsō Peninsula. On it stood a small cabin that he intended to tear down to make room for some grandiose real estate project he had in mind. But already the real estate bubble had burst and it was unlikely that he would ever find the wealthy investors to finance his ambitious scheme.

The cabin itself was a very modest affair: just an eight-*tatami* room that could be split in half by two *fusuma*, a small kitchenette with a wide stainless-steel sink and a tiny bathroom with a stainless-steel bathtub just large enough to sit in with one's legs pulled up to one's chest. Yet it was all I needed, and for the next six weeks, I spent my days in happy seclusion, working on my thesis on Japanese journalism in the mornings and resting and reading in the afternoon and evening.

Around noon I would either go swimming or walking. A steep and semi-hardened road, its sides littered with rubbish—washing machines, rice cookers, and other discarded domestic appliances—led down to the rocky coast. Towards the south, there was a long concrete sea wall. But towards the north, only some fifty yards from where the road terminated in a wide blob of concrete, was a stretch of sandy beach facing a small island, its crest dense with trees and shrubs.

It was only March and the sea was still icy cold, but I made it a point to go swimming whenever the sun was out. On cloudy days, I would go on long walks, following the rugged coast for miles. Toward the south, the boulder-strewn beach ended under a high headland crowned by a lighthouse that cast its seeking beam over a restless sea at night. Toward the north the beach was more accessible, much of it black sand and some scattered rock formations, which was probably the reason why the expensive villas built during the booming eighties—but which now stood mostly vacant—encroached upon the shore with increasing frequency.

Invariably cast in clinically white ferroconcrete and mirrored windows, I imagined these sinister dwellings, jutting out over the Pacific's emerald swell like German bunkers over the Atlantic, to be the kind of hideouts owned by men like Joji Obara, the notorious serial rapist now sitting out a life sentence for abducting and raping hundreds of Asian and Western women.

A naturalized Japanese of Korean descent, Joji's father had started out as an impoverished scrap collector who had finally made it big in the pachinko and taxi trade. Joji and his brothers had enjoyed a secluded childhood with private tuition, and had come into great wealth at the age of seventeen when his father passed away. Graduating from Keio University with degrees in politics and law, he began to invest in real estate and quickly made himself a fortune during the roaring eighties. He lost most of it again when the bubble burst during the early nineties, after which he is said to have used his firm as a laundering front for the Sumiyoshi-kai *yakuza* syndicate.

As early as the late sixties he had begun his sordid career of violating women, luring them to his seaside apartment in Zushi, at the foot of the Miura Peninsula. There he spiked their drinks with Rohypnol, or he simply doused them with chloroform. By the middle of the nineties, he had by his own admission 'conquerplayed' more than two hundred women. By the end of the decade, he had already appeared on the radar of the authorities, though mainly for secretly taking photographs in women's toilets.

Joji Obara was finally arrested in October 2000 in the

wake of the disappearance of Lucie Blackman, a hostess at one of Roppongi's many nightclubs, whom he had taken on a *dōhan*, a paid date. Four months later, on February 9, 2001, her remains were found in a shallow grave under a discarded bathtub in a cave along the shore of the Miura Peninsula, just a few hundred meters below his seaside apartment. Her body had been cut into eight parts with a chainsaw and her severed head had been shaved and cast in concrete. During subsequent searches of his apartment, the police recovered as many as four thousand videotapes chronicling hundreds of date rapes. They also found journals in which he justified his utilitarian approach to women, writing they were 'only good for sex,' mere tools through whom he sought to exact his 'revenge on the world.'

Not all the dwellings along the Taitō Misaki coast were as sinister. One, a small house made of wood, was the home of an old English veteran of the Second World War. I had run into him on my return from the local grocery store. He was driving an old Land Rover, one of the old grey-blue ones with the set-back grille. Pulling up along the side of the road he had addressed me, asking me where I was from and what I was up to. When I said I was from Holland and working on my thesis, he said I should come over for a beer some evening.

Roger had been part of the allied forces and had stayed on after the allied occupation had ended in 1952. Since then he had been in charge of the upkeep of British war cemeteries in Japan.

We talked till late in the night. When I was about to leave he asked me if I had visited the small local temple yet. I said no. 'Then you should,' he said, 'since you're reading at Waseda. Its founder Ōkuma Shigenobu had a *bessō* near here. It has long since disappeared, but the temple still houses his wife's palanquin. They say that, whilst on holiday here, his wife was bitten by a snake and died, and that he never visited Taitō Misaki again.'

It was on one of my long walks along the coast, three weeks before I was due to return to Tokyo to commence my studies, that I came upon a litter of three screaming kittens along the side of the road. They had obviously just been abandoned by someone—casually cast from a quickly opened car door by a cold-hearted owner—for it had been drizzling all day and they were still relatively dry. So for the next three weeks, I had three feline companions, tickling me awake with their whiskers in the morning and sending me off to sleep during my afternoon *hirune* (siesta) with their purring as they huddled together on my chest. One week before I had to leave, I took their photo and hung up copies around restaurants and shops throughout the area with a notice saying they needed a kind owner as a matter of urgency. As luck would have it an unmarried truck driver living on his own responded and decided to take the whole litter.

Thankfully, not all single men living along the coast here were like Joji Obara.

Kamakura

I had never been to Kamakura before and its ancient sites were a welcome antidote to the modern sprawl between Tokyo and Yokohama. A temple town by origin, Kamakura rose to prominence during the reign of Minamoto no Yoritomo, Japan's first military dictator. It was he who, in 1192, turned it into the country's de facto capital by making it the seat of his Bakufu, and whose remains are still buried not far from the Hachiman temple.

Given its rich history, already during the Edo period, Kamakura became a popular tourist destination, its famed Hachiman temple and Daibutsu advertised by the woodblock prints of Andō Hiroshige and others.

The first foreigners to visit the town during the closing decades of the nineteenth century found the town very much as it had been for centuries.

Lafcadio Hearn, who visited Kamakura for the day while still staying at Yokohama following his arrival in Japan, extensively toured the place with his guide Akira, and described in his inimitable mysterious way his visit to the Hase-*dera*, where he marveled at the thirty feet high golden statue of Kannon:

Then the old priest lights a lantern, and leads the way, through a low doorway on the left of the altar, into the interior of the temple, into some very lofty darkness. I follow him cautiously awhile, discerning nothing but the flicker of the lantern. Then we halt before something which gleams. A moment, and my eyes, becoming more accustomed to the darkness, begin to distinguish outlines. The gleaming object defines itself gradually as a foot, an immense golden foot, and I perceive the hem of a golden robe undulating over the instep. Now the other foot appears; the figure is certainly standing. I can perceive that we are in a narrow but also very lofty chamber, and that out of some mysterious blackness overhead ropes are dangling down into the circle of lantern light illuminating the golden feet. The priest lights two more lanterns, and suspends them on hooks attached to a pair of pendant ropes about a yard apart; then he pulls up both together slowly. More of the golden robe is revealed as the lanterns ascend, swinging on their way; then the outlines of two mighty knees; then the curving of columnar thighs under chiseled drapery, and, as with the still waving ascent of the lanterns the golden vision towers ever higher through the gloom, expectation intensifies. There is no sound but the sound of the invisible pulleys overhead, which squeak like bats. Now above the golden girdle, the suggestion of a bosom. Then the glowing of a golden hand uplifted in benediction. Then another golden hand holding a lotus. And at last a face, golden, smiling with eternal youth and infinite tenderness, the face of Kannon.

Next on his stop is the Kamakura Daibutsu, the massive copper statue of Buddha:

You do not see the Daibutsu as you enter the grounds of his long-vanished temple, and proceed along a paved path across stretches of lawn; great trees hide him. But very suddenly, at a turn, he comes into full view and you start! No matter how many photographs of the colossus you may have already seen, this first vision of the reality is an astonishment. Then you imagine that you are already too near, though the image is at least a hundred yards away. As for me, I retire at once thirty or forty yards back, to get a better view. And the *jinrikisha* man runs after me, laughing and gesticulating, thinking that I imagine the image alive and am afraid of it.

Another foreigner to see the Daibutsu was Marie Carmichael Stopes, the brilliant British palaeobotanist and (more controversially) fervent eugenics advocate:

> The principal sight of the place is the great Daibutsu, or gigantic metal statue of a seated Buddha. Most Japanese Buddhas are travesties of nature and abominations of art—but this one compels reverence and attracts devotion. Its stillness (a stillness far greater than that of a house, a statue, or any ordinary inanimate thing), its great size and the wonderful calm on the face, the beautiful human lips and broad-based nose, all make one dream and presently drop a tear or two if no one is looking. Several of us went together by day to see it—but in the evening I slipped off alone to its little grove and saw it in the starlight. Unfortunately, there was no moon that night.

Another attraction was—and still is—the small island of Enoshima:

> It is perfectly exquisite. The island is connected with the mainland by a very long narrow bridge of rickety planks, over the mile of sand which may be covered by the tide, or may be dry, according as the sand drifts year by year. The little island is very steeply hilly and well-wooded and is laid out in long flights of stone

steps up and down the hills, leading to the numerous temples and shrines. It is a sacred island, sacred to the goddess of Luck (and a few others), and except for bazaars, where wonderful shells are sold, and the houses for the pilgrims to rest in, there is almost nothing but temples and shrines on the island. At every turn of the pathway, something quaint or pretty meets the eye, while the views out to sea, across to the mainland and other islands, are magnificent. Going across the bridge homeward the wind was so strong that we were nearly blown off it several times, but the waves were grand, and a heavy rainstorm added to the effect.

Where Kamakura has retained much of its beauty because it and its temples are nestled among the hills, Enoshima and the coast around it has fallen prey to the ever-encroaching need for mobility, convenience, additional attractions. It seems the innate beauty and history of these places are no longer enough to satisfy the tourist's voracious appetite for 'entertainment'. Now an aquarium, light-up displays, and a 'sea candle' are called on to divert adults from the worries of modern-day life and to remedy the short attention span of their easily bored children.

Ogawa-san

I had read the sign, 'Due to recent thefts of personal valuables, we urge our visitors to use the coin lockers at all times.' But I had no faith in keys (even Japanese ones), and decided I would keep a watchful eye on my basket through the stained glass window that separated the dressing room from the bath-room. I could tell by the single filled plastic basket on the shelves the bath was occupied by just one person. But then again, it only took one person to steal one's possessions.

Thus obsessing about my iPhone and wallet being stolen, I took off my clothes and entered the *furo*. Sitting on the side of the bath was a man I presumed to be in his late sixties. I walked over to the showers and sat down on one of the low plastic stools to rinse myself down before entering the bath but couldn't help noticing the man staring at me, though I couldn't quite make out with what purpose.

Having washed myself down, I entered the bath when he suddenly asked, 'Has it been hot here lately?' I thought it an odd question coming from a native, but politely obliged by giving him my take on the weather. I asked whether he had heard the latest about the eruption threat of Mt. Hakone, as I was planning to cross the pass the next day. He said he didn't know, as he had been abroad, to the Philippines, to be precise. I now understood his earlier question and nodded in understanding.

'I'm married to a Philippine, you see,' he said almost rhetorically now. 'I suppose it's quite remarkable, given the way we behaved over there during the Second World War. I know the German Nazis did appalling things too, but the Germans at least have seriously reflected on their war crimes. That's something utterly absent here in Japan.'

I proffered it was partly to blame on the Japanese Ministry of Education, who have stubbornly resisted repeated attempts by prominent Japanese scholars to include the darker episodes of Japanese history in their high school text-books.

'That's true,' he said. 'We focus far too much on acquiring knowledge, far too little on fostering wisdom.'

I remained silent: what could one say in the face of that?

'It seems we don't reflect at all on our purpose in life. There is no serious thought about what constitutes personal happiness, what it means to be a good human being. How rewarding it is to help one's fellow man, however tiny that contribution might be,' he said, pincering an imaginary grain of rice between his thumb and index fingers.

'I was at Sagamihara, south of Tokyo, when the great earthquake of 2011 struck the Tōhoku region and thought the house was collapsing. In the wake of the tsunami there was a great demand for assistance in rebuilding the area. I applied for a two-year assignment to come and help out.

'My specialty is urban development, especially making hitherto uninhabited mountainous regions inhabitable. At first it felt good. I thought I was making a difference. There was no lack of funds and they surely talked the talk. But I soon realized there was no policy in place whatsoever as to how to go about the immense task. Worse still, they kept wasting money on ill-conceived plans, like the proverbial bathwater'—he splashed some of it over the edge of the bath—'just so they could show they were making an effort. It felt as if they didn't really care what happened on the ground, as long as they looked good in the media.

'I tried to do something to correct it, but of course I was sidetracked, which is the usual way we deal with difficult people: we don't fire them, we immobilize them.'

In Ogawa-*san*'s view it was all part and parcel of the wider corruption among politicians and the higher echelons of the civil service—a total disconnect with the wishes and needs of the populace and a stunning ability to gloss over or even purposefully cover up injustices when it served their own interests. A case in point was the recent political scandal in which the Ministry of Agriculture had used scaly statistical methods to shortchange the recipients of unemployment and compensation benefits to the tune of sixty billion yen.

'Is it any wonder,' he said as he looked at me hopelessly, 'that people have come to believe there are just two groups in society, the *kachigumi* and the *makegumi*, the winners and the losers—no in-between, just winners and losers. And it is money and possessions that determine to which of the two groups you belong.'

I felt a pang of shame at my earlier misgivings about my things being stolen. Here was Ogawa-*san* sitting on the edge of the bath pondering the increasing materialism of his countrymen, while on the other side of the stained glass window I had been stressing he might steal my precious iPhone.

We had been silent for a while when he asked me what I did for a living. I told him I wrote books on Japanese topics, specifically Japan's middle ages.

'Do you know the story of *Chūshingura*?' he asked, his eyes suddenly lighting up. I said I did. It was the story of the forty-seven loyal retainers, who had avenged their lord, Asano Naganori, by killing the man who caused his downfall. That man was Kira Yoshinaka, a prominent Bakufu court official whose role it had been to instruct the rural lord in the niceties of court etiquette. This was called for, as Naganori had been appointed master of ceremony during an upcoming visit by envoys of the imperial court in Kyoto. But the arrangement went horribly wrong when, following an altercation between the two, Naganori stabbed

Yoshinaka in the face. Though the latter was hardly wounded, Naganori was forced to commit *seppuku*—to draw one's weapon at the Shōgun's court was inexcusable. The story is hugely popular in Japan and has featured in countless stage plays, novels, films, and television dramas.

'And why do you think it is still so popular?'

I said I thought it was a typical story about loyalty.

'I see,' he said, tilting his head as if pondering my answer. Then he said he thought there might be yet another reason. He thought it was the sense of injustice. It was true that the Asano retainers were fiercely loyal, but what had driven them in their act was their outrage at the way their lord had been treated. It was true their lord had drawn his weapon on Yoshinaka, but he had only done so after Yoshinaka had openly insulted him for being a country bumpkin. Having one's dignity offended in such a manner, they argued, was reason enough for their lord to draw his weapon.

Yet their real outrage lay with the unjust way in which the authorities had dealt with the matter. Instead of punishing both parties for disturbing the peace at the Shōgunal court, they had singled out their lord to set an example and quickly close the matter. Meanwhile, the prominent Bakufu official, undoubtedly because of his connections at court, had been let off scot-free.

Ogawa-*san* himself, incidentally, had been born in a small village overlooking the ruins of Akō castle, the former residence of Lord Asano and had grown up with the story.

It was the same sense of frustration with the wider injustices in this world that had made Tora-*san* such a hit in his time, he believed. Tora-*san* is the hero of the film-series *Otoko wa tsurai yo* (*It's Tough Being a Man*), spanning 48 installments and running for more than two and a half decades. Tora-*san* is a kind-hearted vagabond, invariably unlucky in love and always hoping to make it big. Only recently they had made another installment, which was set for release later this year. Yet he believed it would probably be a one-off, and he feared that the viewer's waning interest did not bode well for the way the country was going.

'I suppose it's not much different in Germany and the UK, though I don't hear much news of corruption cases from your country, he said wistfully.'

I assured him we had had our fair share of scandals in Holland too. And though we might not have conducted wars of aggression like Japan and Germany, our colonial history was far from unblemished, if such a thing were even possible. It was only recently that some of the more blatant atrocities we had committed in our unsuccessful attempts to suppress the Indonesian independence movement during the late nineteen forties had received proper attention in the media, though they had come to light decades ago. Some one-hundred thousand Indonesians lost their lives in that struggle, many of them civilians. One particularly gruesome incident occurred in the south Celebes over Christmas, 1946, when a Dutch battalion indiscriminately slaughtered some four thousand Indonesians over a two-month period. Even the Germans had the decency to climb out of their trenches during the First World War to celebrate the coming of Christ with their enemies. In one of those incredible twists of historical irony that would sound far-fetched in fiction, our soldiers committed these atrocities even while our judges were sitting in judgment over the Germans at Nuremberg and the Japanese at Tokyo. Volume upon volume had been written about the horrors of life under German occupation, or under Japanese occupation in Indonesia, for that matter. Yet when it came to the suffering of Indonesians over countless generations under the Dutch imperialist yoke we seemed to suffer from general amnesia. Needless to say, I hadn't come across any of this in my high school textbooks when I was young, nor did I entertain any illusions it had found its way there since.

'I've read Anne Frank's diary when I was young,' he said, 'though I confess I bought the book thinking it was an erotic work.' He laughed heartily, but in an honest and disarming way, about his youthful foolishness, not unlike Tora-*san* would have.

I asked him why he thought Anne Frank's diary was such a huge hit in Japan, especially among young Japanese women.

'It's the same isn't it: the sense of injustice. Women in Japan, especially young women, are in a vulnerable position. And isn't it during times of war and occupation that such vulnerabilities are thrown into sharp relief?'

I couldn't help but feel embarrassed again. Here was I, a professed writer, and I was being given profound insights into the human condition by the first best man I encountered during a soak in a bath in a capsule hotel in Fujisawa. Ogawa-*san* might be worried about the moral decline of his fellow countrymen, but I would be hard put to give one single instance in which I had ever had such a conversation with a perfect stranger in my own country. He might be worried nevertheless, but as long as I had such encounters in Japan—as I've often had—I wasn't too worried about where the average Japanese person was heading.

Onsen

I spent the eve of my ascent of the Hakone Pass at the comfortable yet very affordable Plum Hostel in Odawara in the company of three Japanese Hell's Angels. Well, not really. They certainly looked the part and rode Harley Davidsons. But, this being Japan, they were all perfect gentlemen.

'We're from Okinawa and on our way to Tokyo,' one of them told me as he donned his military-style helmet and hoisted himself out of his leather gear and chains. I said I had never been to Okinawa but would love to see it someday. At this he seemed delighted and bowed deeply, his back as straight as an ironing board, and his hand and fist reverently joined together as if he were a Shaolin monk. Then, without rising, he grabbed my hand with both hands to shake it ever so gently.

They spent the evening out on the town but, even though we shared the same room, I never heard them return and slept like a rose.

Setting out for Hakone the next morning after plenty of coffee, I passed Odawara castle, its donjon's brilliant white upper story towering over the verdant trees. Once this castle had been the headquarters of the powerful Hōjō clan. How impressive it must have looked to the medieval traveler.

I had by now developed a nasty blister on one of my toes, and to avoid its bursting I decided to stop for the night at Yumoto, or 'Source of Hot Water.'

I found a nice hostel called Guest House Azito, with friendly staff and affordable prices. They had Japanese-style rooms, but since I was traveling alone I decided to again go for one of the capsules, which were located in a three-storied annex. 'Capsule' was an understatement really. They weren't the usual plastic cocoons, but hand-built wooden cabins stacked two stories high and containing a double-sized mattress.

This was *onsen* (hot spring) territory, and the staff recommended the Hakone no Yū, which was a ten-minute walk up the road and cost only five hundred yen if one purchased an entry ticket through them.

The *onsen* was nothing over the top but nice enough, with several hot baths in varying grades of temperature and vistas of pine-covered slopes through the mountain mist. I chose the least hot bath, as it had been a sultry day and I was pretty hot already. The *yū*, or hot well water, gurgled up through a massive rock at the corner of the bath. At first, it looked contrived, but looking closer I could see the water had gouged deep crevices into the surface of the rock, laying bare its layers in a variety of hues, suggesting it had coursed through them for ages.

Some of the water was conducted through bamboo piping to create a double-barreled shower that poured down in narrow jets. I moved under to let them clatter down on my back, when an elderly man, lean and tanned, took hold of my shoulders and moved them back to pinpoint the jets at specific positions right above my shoulder blades. 'That's the right way,' he said, 'it's good for your health.' I presumed he was referring to the pressure points used in *shiatsu*, and wondered whether all Japanese had this innate knowledge of traditional healing. The man's high brow was set in a perpetual kind of reversed frown, which lent his face an intelligent look but made it appear as if he was in a constant state of bewildered perplexity.

When I had had enough and was about to leave, I saw the same man standing next to a large trough, scooping up big ladles of water and pouring it over himself. I asked him what was its purpose.

'It's to condition our body. Unlike the Scandinavians, we don't believe in the cold water shock treatment. You being young can easily adjust, but for elderly people like me it is better to first pour some hot water over ourselves to let our bodies adjust to the heat.'

Then he looked slightly vexed. 'Did you see that man put the ladle down? That's completely wrong! You're never supposed to place it flat down. It's bad bathing etiquette. This is how you put it down,' he said, as he gently took up the ladle in question and rested it against the rim of the trough so the water could drip off properly. 'There are many rules that govern the ritual of bathing, but most of them are meant to make the experience as wholesome as possible. Thus you should never stay in a hot bath for longer than twenty minutes. After that, you should at least take a ten-minute break. And when you do, always do so upwind.'

I looked puzzled.

'See the steam rising from the hot bath?' he said as he looked at it meaningfully. 'See how it drifts away from us and not towards us? That's how it should be. You should try and inhale as little of the vapors as possible. The waters are wholesome to the body, and even the vapors, to a certain extent. But to inhale too much of them is a bad thing—as are all things taken to excess. They contain all kinds of wholesome ingredients, but inevitably, coming from where they come, they also contain toxins. It is like medicine: too much of it will kill you.'

I nodded in agreement. I once took two hundred paracetamol tablets. It wasn't a pleasant experience.

Throne

Two years passed after my year at Waseda University before I saw Japan again. Having graduated from university back home, I did a short stint as a technical translator at a Japanese car factory near Maastricht. But my heart wasn't in it and that winter, I moved in with Nadja, who was still studying Japanese in Bonn. For the next year, I lived in Germany, spending three days a week working at the *Doitsu nyūsu dai-jesuto*, a weekly Japanese-language newspaper for Japanese expats living in Germany. The rest of the week, I worked on my first proper book, an elaboration on my thesis on Japanese journalism. I wasn't sure yet what I was going to do after that, but for the time being, I was happy: Germany was interesting and life was good.

But after a year in Germany, our relationship broke down, and I had to decide what to do next. I had finished my book and was eager to get back to Japan and immerse myself in Japanese life and culture. To do that, I reckoned, I had to live and work in Japan for at least a few years. How long exactly remained an open question.

And so I boarded the plane to Japan again. I stayed with my German friend Gero, who was still researching his doctoral thesis and now lived in a tiny apartment near Roppongi.

After a month of scanning the classified adds of the major newspapers, I finally landed myself a job in Japan, the requirement for obtaining a working visa. To apply, I had to go to a Japanese embassy abroad. Theo, a Dutch university friend of mine, who had studied Chinese and economy, had landed a job with a Dutch dairy company operating in China and he and his future wife, Hanneke, were living on a compound for foreigners in Beijing.

I stayed with them for a week, plenty of time to apply for a visa, and sufficient to see most of the sights. It was good to see them again, but I noticed how, after just one year in China, Theo was already swearing at cab drivers and hotel staff, albeit in Dutch. It was there and then that I decided that if I were ever to reach this point in Japan, I would pack up my belongings and go home.

Thanks to Japanese efficiency the visa application was a breeze, and I spent the remainder of my time visiting the major sites: the Great Wall, the Temple of Heaven, and of course the Imperial Palace.

Not wanting to rely on my limited knowledge of just written Chinese, I rented an audio guide in English. I switched it on and heard a familiar voice: 'Hello. My name is Roger Moore, and for the next hour I will be your guide to the magnificent Forbidden City.' It was slightly odd hearing the suave voice associated worldwide with 007, the spy in Her Majesty's Service, guiding me around the Forbidden City—as if it were a giant theme park of the Bond franchise.

The tour was fascinating enough. The wide forecourt where embassies of foreign kings and queens had presented their tribute, the endless corridors and rooms for the vast army of eunuchs that kept the palace running, the luxurious quarters of the emperor's many concubines: each was more impressive than the other. My interest was only dampened by a growing nausea—obviously the Peking Duck my friend had treated me to the previous night had not gone down well.

I was about to enter the audience room with the ??? imperial throne when I felt my bowels make a sudden lurch, as if a plug had been pulled, followed by a cold shiver running down my spine. Rushing outside, toward the row of primitive toilets on the edge of the compound, I pulled the wooden door shut behind me, unbuttoned my trousers as fast as I could, and sat down to let nature take its course.

Relieved I had made it in time, I reached for the toilet paper, when the rickety roller came loose, causing the paper roll to jump toward the floor. I made a last valiant lurch for the roll in midair but had to look on helplessly as it fell to the ground and disappeared through the high opening under the door. Stooping forward from my toilet seat, yet fearful to soil myself, I tried to haul the roll in by its paper trail, only succeeding in sending the darn thing farther away from me. On the other side of the door, I began to hear Chinese calling to each other in merriment: they had obviously noted what was happening and having a swell time. Agitated, I began to pull harder when my elbow activated the audio guide now dangling between my legs: '—And now you finally find yourself in the most hallowed room of the Forbidden City, the inner sanctum, the center of the realm. Here, from this very seat, generations of emperors have ruled over an empire whose borders stretched from the mountains of Afghanistan to the Yellow Sea, from the deserts of Mongolia to the island province of Hainang. Now just take a moment and imagine yourself in their place—imagine the power that comes with occupying this throne of thrones, this seat of heaven.'

Hakone

Along the road to Hakone, I passed a narrow slab of rock, placed upright at the entrance to a side path of the road inscribed with the characters Wariishi-*zaka* (severed rock slope). A wooden sign placed alongside it read:

> It is said that this is the place where Soga Gorō, who was on his way to the foot of Mount Fuji to slay an enemy, cut a massive rock in two, so as to test the cut of the sword he was wearing.

Throughout the country, one can find such stones with similar stories attached to them, some as large as a car. Medieval Japan must have been teeming with swordsmen testing their weapon on the first best rock they encountered on their way to their duel. Or perhaps it was just littered with rocks split by the forces of nature, as well as a lot of people with a vivid imagination.

A bit farther on there was another sign. This one was about the Tendai monk, Shinran Shōnin. It read:

On his return from the eastern countries, having completed his work of spreading the faith, Shōnin and four of his disciples came to this place climbing the steep Hakone road, when Shōnin turned to his disciples Seishin-bō and Ren'i-bō and said, 'I am worried as to who will lead our followers in the eastern countries when you return with me to the capital, and thus I want you to go back and spread the faith.' Having thus implored them, the master and his disciples are said to have sorrowfully taken leave of each other's company.

What the sign failed to mention was that Shinran had not gone north voluntarily, but had been sent there in exile when, in 1207, two of his fellow monks had been caught taking the *nenbutsu*, or Buddha mindfulness practice, to a whole new level by engaging in sex acts—an admittedly pleasantly effective way of staying in 'the now.' Given that background, I wondered in what way exactly his disciples intended to help spread the faith in the eastern countries.

I was now walking the Hatajuku Ichirizuka, a restored stretch of the old Tōkaido between Hatajuku and Hakone. It wasn't long before I ran into a large group of elementary school pupils. They were all wearing *waratabi*, the traditional straw sandals, and being directed up the steep cobbled path by a cadre of teachers armed with high-tech cameras and video recorders. Obviously, this was part of an excursion to experience what it had been like to have to cross the pass under medieval conditions. Luckily they weren't required to do the whole stretch in this manner. A few hundred yards higher up, the teachers were collecting the sandals for next year's excursion.

Their pupils greeted me with the usual 'herooo!' and I complimented them on their stamina.

Armies of up to fifty thousand men once used to climb these steps to traverse these mountains. And they did so at incredible speeds. Thus it took Ieyasu and his army just two days to cross the Hakone Pass when, in the late summer of 1600, he marched down from Edo to Sekigahara in order to fight and defeat the coalition of Japan's western warlords. In that time I would be happy to make it to the top of the pass.

And I was walking the easy route! Ieyasu and his men would still have followed the even older old Yuzaka-*michi*, a footpath that largely followed the ridges of the mountains that stood between the post stations of Yumoto and Hakone.

It was because the Yuzaka-*michi* was so treacherous, that, in 1618, the Bakufu in Edo decided to improve this stretch of the Tōkaidō. Abandoning the old mountain path, they built a new road, which followed the valley of the Sukumo River to Hatajuku, and from there up to Hakone.

Farther uphill there were even stretches left of the old steps. These were a remnant of improvements carried out towards the end of the seventeenth century, when the Bakufu invested the princely sum of fourteen hundred *ryō* (roughly one and a half million dollars in today's money) to pave this whole stretch of the Tōkaidō.

Sadly most of this section of the old highroad was destroyed in the Great Kantō (1923) and North Izu (1930) earthquakes, but its huge flagstones have been used to repave some sections.

One mile before Hakone and Lake Aso I stopped at the Amazake Chaya. It had been recommended to me by Matsuoka-*san*, the kind owner of Hostel House Plum in Odawara. It was a traditional tea house, or *chaya*, but this one also served *amazake*, a sweet, low-alcohol beverage made by a fermenting process using the *kōji* mold.

The Amazake Chaya was certainly worth the stop. The building was more than four hundred years old. It had been in a very poor state when the current owners took it over, but they had it restored to its former glory, along with the beautiful open fireplace with a raised floor. It was a similar structure as the tea house I had visited halfway from Magome to Tsumago along the Nakasendō.

The place was run by a young couple. Matsumoto-*san* was the thirteenth generation owner, a soft-spoken and modest man. I told him I was walking the Nakasendō, and

he gave me a slip of Japanese paper. Written on in bold cal-
ligraphic characters were the words *dōchū anzen*. It was a
paper talisman, whishing travelers a 'safe journey.'

His wife told me that the forty-seven loyal retainers
Ogawa-*san* and I had reminisced about, had stopped here
on their way to Edo to avenge their master. It was—so the
legend went—while resting at the Amazake Chaya that one
of them, a swordsman by the name of Kamizaki Yogorō,
was approached by a packhorse driver offering his service.
Yogorō declined politely—as *samurai* were wont to. But the
driver wouldn't take no for an answer and began to hurl all
kinds of insults at the stoic warrior. For just a moment the
proud *samurai* lost his temper. Bringing his hands to the hilt
of his longsword, he made ready to cut down the insolent
commoner. But then he checked himself and though of the
grave task that lay ahead. And kneeling down deep in front
of the bewildered packhorse driver the *samurai* apologized
instead. Weeks had passed, when news of Kira Yoshinaka's
assassination reached Hakone. It was only then, after Yogorō
and his forty-six fellow retainers had avenged their lord and
committed *seppuku*, that the packhorse driver realized he
had insulted a man who was making ready to meet his end.
To repent he took the tonsure and spent the rest of his life
honoring Yogorō's spirit.

Hakone itself had a laid-back, resort-like feel to it, not unlike
Niko, Ise, and Nara. Busload after busload of old age

pensioners was being ferried in, the passenger dispersing in groups towards their hotels of destination. On Lake Aso small swan-shaped paddling boats drifted across the smooth water, the only ripple caused by the coming and going of the ferry that tours the lake. On its eastern shore tourists climbed the long flight of stairs to the ancient Hakone shrine, which dates back to the middle of the eighth century. The whole place breathed nostalgia, a world at ease with itself, like an early Technicolor scene from a bygone era.

I had hoped to find a place to stay for the night, but unfortunately, the one slightly affordable place was fully booked—and this on a weekday outside of Golden Week! It seemed I wasn't the only one seeking a bit of quietude.

Simply the Best

I had landed myself a job and had applied for my visa, but I still had to wait three months for the mill of Japanese bureaucracy to process my application before I would actually be able to start working.

As always, my Japanese family was eager to help out, but this time they weren't in the position to offer me any work. The boom years of the eighties were a thing of the past and it was late summer, the least busy time of the year for a scroll maker. This meant I couldn't help Teruo-*san* out in the shop to earn my living, as I had done when I had lived with them in 1989.

Luckily, Teruo-san did know someone who could use an extra hand: Koyama-san, the owner of the small house near Taitō Misaki where I had written my thesis on Japanese journalism. He was one of Teruo-san's old high school friends and now ran his own building company from his home town of Onjuku, a coastal town on the east coast of the Bōsō Peninsula and only half an hour by car from Mōbara, where the Takayanagis lived.

Unlike most Japanese Koyama-*san* was a larger-than-life character; he had something of Genghis Kahn about him, both in the way he looked and in the brazenness of his exploits. One of them was his almost fatal crash with his private Cessna airplane. Another was his near-death experience by preparing a *sashimi* dish from the fearsome *fugu*, or blowfish, one of the most poisonous fish on the market. Only a select group of chefs are allowed to prepare the dish for paying customers, but only after they have passed the most grueling of exams after three years of training. Even in spite of this, every year half a dozen Japanese die the most agonizing death—one's muscles are paralyzed—by eating only the tiniest quantity of the lethal poison tetrodotoxin, one fish carrying enough to kill more than people. Most of them are foolhardy types like Koyama-*san*, who think they can do it without the proper training. Koyama-*san*, of course, survived, but his mouth had been numb for several days.

Koyama-*san*'s company wasn't a huge operation. There was a chic head office on Onjuku's high street. But the sawmill and wood storage was in a huge ramshackle shed behind his house, just a short stroll away from the rolling surf.

Koyama-*san*'s house was more like a mansion, really. It was one of those old-style villas in the *irimoya* tradition, its roof clad in the classic grey enamel tiles that bore the family crest along the foot of its wide eaves. The floors of its many rooms were covered with *tatami* mats that had seen better days but lent the place a less formal atmosphere than had they been new. I was allotted an upstairs, eight-*tatami* room, and for the next three months, I lived with the Koyama—him, his wife and their two sons—like I was part of the family, as I had with the Takayanagis seven years before.

Six days a week we got up at six in the morning and after a hearty Japanese breakfast of rice, *miso* soup, roasted fish, and pickles, we would load up the trucks with the required tools and materials and head towards our respective *genba*, or building sites.

The *genba* I was assigned to was to become an OM Solar House, the Japanese equivalent to Germany's *Passivhaus*. 'O' stands for *omoshiroi* (interesting) and 'M' for *mottainai* (too good to be wasted), i.e., to let no energy go to waste, but in an ingenious way. Its main feature was a south-facing roof with a hollow structure, allowing hot air ascending along the house's white walls to be sucked in through air ducts in the eaves and rise to the top of the roof. There it would be sent through a dedicated handling unit (the most expensive part of the house) to warm the household water. In summer the excess hot air could be released through the roof, but in winter it would be sent down through a vertical duct to eventually warm the interior through vents in the downstairs floor. Koyama-*san* had already built a number of these houses. And he was one of many. By now Japan can boast some twenty-five thousand of these energy-neutral houses.

His workforce consisted of a hardy dozen carpenters, old hands, who were from the area and all conversed in the local dialect. It wasn't all that different from standard Japanese, but it was littered with 'd's and 'p's, and to a fresh graduate like me, who wasn't even familiar with all the technical terms, it posed an extra hurdle.

I tried hard to catch up. And like them, I wore the regular carpenter's attire, with the baggy trousers and tight cotton boots with the flimsy soles. It was only now that I appreciated how suitable they were for the work we were doing: through the thin soles one could feel exactly where one was treading, while the single toe provided extra grip when one had to tightrope the narrow beams of the house's upper structure to tighten some bolt or hand someone a tool. Had I worn the bulky safety shoes from back home I would most likely have ended up plummeting to an early death.

I had already experienced the culture of Japanese crafts-manship while working as a *deshi* (apprentice) in Teruo-*san*'s small workshop. But here, working among this hardy bunch of carpenters, I was again struck by the dignity and calm with which they worked alongside each other. There was none of the loud swearing you could hear on a Dutch building site. Most of the day they would work away in silence, only exchanging a few words when guiding a beam into place or discussing a technical issue. The predominant sound was that of their tools, the saw, the hammer and chisel, the occasional power tool. Sometimes someone would set in a song. Then the others would chime in, usually just with some refrain: '*dappe yo, dappe yo, dappe yo!*'

Nor was there any of the shoddy work one was used to back home. All of Koyama-*san*'s labor core were tradition-ally-schooled carpenters, with long, long years of hard apprenticeship under their belts. And though we were building a modern house using modern construction tech-niques, they approached their work with the same dedication and finesse had they been sawing and chiseling the intricate joinery in which they had been trained.

At noon, the simple *bentō* lunch was usually enjoyed in silence, but occasionally one of them would tell an anecdote or joke that would be greeted with copious laughter.

I had worked for Koyama-*san* for a month. Autumn was approaching, and with increasing frequency typhoons began to sweep in from the Pacific to hit the Japanese mainland.

I still remember one Sunday in October. It was pouring down in buckets, the wind was howling around the house, and the windows were rattling. I was enjoying my one day off, reading in my room, when I heard Koyama-*san* calling me from downstairs. 'Let's go!' he shouted, 'One of the roof covers has come undone.' Putting on raincoats we rushed into the yard and jumped into one of the parked trucks. It was half an hour's drive to the *genba* in question and along the route, we could see the havoc the typhoon was wreaking. Palm trees were being uprooted, broken roof tiles lay strew across the road, and sheets of corrugated iron that had been ripped off sheds were flying around like discarded newspaper sheets. Here and there you could see a person trying to reach safety, leaning into the wind as if standing on the sloping deck of a heaving ship, or skidding along on their backs behind inverted umbrellas. By the time we reached the building site the huge tarpaulin that had covered the uncompleted roof had all but detached itself. Hamstrung by only a few ropes at one corner, the thick and sturdy canvas was now fiercely batting and flapping in the gale-force winds, bludgeoning the scaffolding around the house as if it were made of chopsticks. It was truly terrifying.

'You stay in the truck,' Koyama-*san* shouted above the roaring gale. 'If something happens to me, get help.' Then he grabbed a long, coiled up rope from behind his seat, jumped out of the cabin, slung it around his neck, and began to climb the scaffolding on the lee side of the house, all the while trying to evade the dangerously lashing canvas. Having made it to the top, he moved to where the canvas was still attached. He tied one end of the rope to the scaffolding, grabbed part of the canvas and, holding it down with incredible strength, threaded the other end through one of the rings in the seam. Then he let the canvas fly again to haul in the rope, bit by bit, as if he were breaking in a bolting horse. He repeated the grueling exercise with the next ring, and the next, until he had worked his way all around the house and the tarpaulin was tied down safe and secure against the scaffolding. It had taken him more than an hour.

When he finally climbed back into the truck, he had a gaping wound above his left brow, which he stemmed by tightly tying a small towel around his head, like a Caribbean pirate.

It was already growing dark by the time we returned, when we hit a section of the road that went through a steep defile. The road had completely gone; instead, there was now a large pool, some twenty yards in diameter, and far too deep to drive even a truck through.

Without thinking twice Koyama-*san* jumped down from the cabin again, took off his shirt and trousers, and waded into the murky water. By the time he neared its center the water was up to his head. He swam a few more yards and then dived under and vanished completely. For a few anxious moments, I waited at the water's edge, mentally preparing myself to dive in after him in case he might not come up again, when he finally rose to the surface, panting hard and holding in his hands a bundle of long grass that had clogged the sewage drain at the bottom of the defile. A few more times he repeated his act, each time casting the debris far away from him. Then he quickly swam back and put his clothes on again.

We stood and watched at the edge of the water as a small ripple appeared at the pool's center. Soon it turned into a huge vortex that drained the pool in a matter of minutes. 'That's why the drainage grates along our roads are so big and sturdy,' Koyama-*san* said, staring at the slurping vortex. 'If not, they would collapse under the strain.'

On another occasion, we went down to help clean up a house that stood in a valley and had likewise been inundated. By the time the water receded, its ground floors were covered in a thick layer of fine sludge that seemed to penetrate everything. We spent the whole day, and the next day, cleaning up the mess and restoring the house to a semblance of what it had been, though most of the furniture was ruined.

I thought the house belonged to a relative or a friend, but I was wrong. It had been built by Koyama-*san*: the Japanese sense of service to one's customers stretched well beyond the purchasing date.

I enjoyed my three months at Koyama-*san*'s building company more than I would the next three years at the robotics company, even though the pay was only a tenth of what I would earn there. And I learned more—more about the mentally of the Japanese worker, their commitment, their modesty, their hardiness, and their overall good humor. Of all my years working for Japanese companies, those three months among that small band of carpenters on the Pacific coast were simply the best.

Nekkutai

Mishima was no different from Japan's other sprawling cities. I found a place to stay for the night in a 'business *ryōkan*.' It had traditional Japanese rooms with *tatami* and a small *furo*, but otherwise, it was a sad affair, the stale air of better times hanging over it like a molded blanket.

Getting up early the next morning, I was just in time to spot some of the other guests, all of them *sararimen*, the ubiquitous Japanese white-collar worker. They were dressed in the uniform of corporate Japan: the nondescript suits in subdued grays and blues, the black leather belt with the cheap square buckle, and of course the *nekkutai*, the subtle but ever-present reminder of the corporate noose around their necks.

I had been asked about my *nekkutai* during my own job interview, some twenty-five years ago. I had landed myself an interview for the position of a technical translator at a robotics company near Nagoya. Furuuchi-*san*, the short and stocky section chief in charge of the translation department, had made me sit for a written test about some mechanical device. I had come through alright, but then he started grilling me about my rather casual appearance. I was wearing khaki trousers and a polo shirt. It was high summer and I just hadn't the inclination or the money to hoist myself into a dark suit and white shirt with its suffocating collar: I had never cared to do so and wasn't planning on starting the habit in this sweltering heat. Especially one aspect of my attire seemed to trouble him as he removed his large seventies-style glasses, patted his sweaty brow with his handkerchief, and stared at me with his beady eyes as if something was seriously wrong. Then he said, '*Nekkutai wa dō shita no?*' (What happened to your necktie?).

It was only much later that I found out it had been my one year at Waseda University that had saved me from rejection. Being from the northern island of Hokkaidō himself, Furuuchi-*san* had been deeply impressed with me entering Waseda, a privilege he could only have dreamt of when he was still a high school student. Founded by Ōkuma Shigenobu, one of Japan's great Meiji statesmen, more than a century ago, Waseda (then still called Tōkyō Senmon Gakkō) is now ranked among Japan's top universities and has been attended by a string of Japanese celebrities, among them former Prime Minister Takeshita Noboru, and the author Murakami Haruki.

Most of the company's foreign translators had previously earned their spurs as English teachers and I was his first applicant who had attended one of Japan's top universities. He probably put down my habit of going around half-undressed to Waseda's somewhat liberal reputation—a reputation that had made people like President Bill Clinton choose Waseda as the venue for a speech during their visit to Japan instead of Tōdai (the university that spawns eighty percent of Japan's politicians and civil servants). Had Furuuchi-*san* known I had utterly failed to pass my second-semester exams he would probably still have hired me—after all, it is getting into university that counts in Japan, not what one does once one is in.

Sake

At Hara, halfway along the Suruga Bay towards Fuji, I had just made a photograph of the place where Hiroshige had painted his Asa no Fuji (Morning Fuji), when I ran—or rather walked—into a section of the road that was being dug up. As usual, there was a *keibi-in*, a traffic guard, a job often done by elderly people when it concerns just minor roadworks. When one of them hailed me over I thought I had done something wrong. But I was mistaken. 'Have you visited the *sake* brewery?'

'Eh, no?'

'Go and check it out. It's just around the corner.'

Not wanting to get into trouble with the law, I dutifully complied and walked the twenty or so yards down the road to pay a visit to the Hakuin Masamune brewery.

There was a small shop at the front end of the brewery. Sliding open one of the doors, I stepped onto the raised floor and was greeted by an old lady behind a small counter. There were a few stools with cushions at the window, and toward one side the brewery's products were on display in a tall glass cabinet: various qualities of *sake* in big bottles and, in pint-sized brown bottles, *amazake*.

Being on the road and on foot, I couldn't afford to carry a whole bottle of *sake*. But one could sample a glass of their *amazake* for two hundred yen, so I ordered myself a glass.

The young woman who poured it explained it was made using *kōji*. When I wanted to know more, she told me to wait and went to the back of the shop and disappeared behind a curtain. Shortly afterward a somewhat corpulent young man came into the shop and greeted me. I complimented him on his *amazake*. 'It's the first time I've had it chilled,' I said.

'That's because the warm stuff isn't really *amazake*,' he said. It's *kasuzake*, which is quite different from *amazake*. *Kasuzake* is essentially a side-product of the *sake*-making process by using the residue or *kasu*, and is usually drunk warm in winter. Real *amazake* is made by a separate fermenting process using the *kōji* mold, the same mold used in making *miso* and soy sauce. And unlike *kasuzake* it is drunk cold. You may probably know how in our *haiku* poems we use seasonal words to indicate spring, summer, autumn or winter. *Amazake* is such a word, and it is invariably used to indicate summer, not winter.

Paper

I hit the jackpot that evening as one only seldom does when traveling. The Nasubi Mt. Fuji Backpackers Hostel in Fuji city was the best place I had found so far, even though it was surrounded by huge factories with towering chimneys painted red and white. It's owner, Kazu-*san*, was the most kindly host one could hope for and that evening, to top it all, he and some of his neighbors had organized a small barbecue on the veranda at the back of the hostel.

Manning the grill was Seiki-*san*, a diminutive and bespectacled young man whose bristly hair stood up in the middle, giving him a youthful appearance.

I remarked on the density of factories in this area and wondered what they might be producing, as their chimneys were so tall. Was it something toxic?

'They are paper mills,' Seiki-*san* explained. 'This is a paper-making region. Traditionally we made *washi* from the fibers of the *mitsumata*, the oriental paper bush. This area was ideally situated, as there was ample clean water from Mount Fuji, while the Tōkaidō made the distribution to the rest of the country easy.'

'So why the high chimneys?' I wondered aloud, 'Isn't paper-making a relatively clean process?'

'For *washi*, yes, but not for modern paper,' he said as he pushed his glasses back up his nose whilst turning the *yakitori* skewers. 'The process requires huge amounts of energy, which is generated by burning the pulp that is a residue of the process. Then there is the bleaching or de-inking process, which creates problems of its own. The chimneys are there to reduce the impact of emissions. After the war, when the industry went through a period of rapid growth, there were high rates of lung cancer among the local population. Another huge problem was the sludge, which is another byproduct of the production process.'

At this, he took out his phone with his one free hand, did some tapping and scrolling, and showed me a picture in sepia colors of the local port. You could only tell it was a port by the poop of an old coaster in the foreground, which seemed to sit in a vast rice paddy of light-brown frothing sludge.

'That picture was taken during the nineteen sixties,' he said. 'All the rivers in the area were like that. It was only later, under pressure from local environmental groups, that things began to change. The local politicians, of course, were in the pockets of the industrialists, but when the government too stepped in they finally brushed up their act. Since then many more improvements have been made, so that today our rivers are clean again.'

'So you work in the industry?'

'Actually, no. I work for Japan Rail, in the tourist section. But in my spare time, I do guided tours of the paper mills, which required me to immerse myself in the material.'

Hiroshige

That early morning, from the elevated graveyard of the Tōkaku temple grounds in Fujikawa, I got a splendid view of a snow-crested Mount Fuji. In the thirty years since I set foot in Japan, I had never seen it this clearly and up close.

Slightly uphill I consulted my Tōkaidō route app when a well-dressed man walked over to me from across the road and asked me if I needed any help. I said I was just looking up the correct route, when he took off his spectacles and, squinting down the road, began to give me detailed directions. I interrupted him and showed him the app on my phone to show him I was following the Tōkaidō towards Kyoto.

'So you will be passing through Yui,' he said, as he put on his spectacles again and peered at the small screen.

I said yes.

'In that case, make sure to pay a visit to the Hiroshige museum, it's worth the while.'

The exhibitions at the Shizuoka City Tokaido Hiroshige Museum of Art were indeed very informative. The general exhibition dealt with the *ukiyo-e* tradition, though given the museum's name, it focussed on Ando Hiroshige's work. It did a good job of explaining his genius, his imagination, his use of repetitive motives, colors, movement, time, seasons.

There was a special exhibition on the importance to the Edo citizen of water and fire as expressed in *ukio-e* art: people washing their feet, warming themselves at a campfire, tapping water from a well, and (combining both themes) bathing themselves in fire-heated bathtubs.

Of particular interest to me was a small exhibition on the requirements for travel along Japan's major highroads. It included a small display of travel accessories, including carrying bags, writing utensils, fire-making equipment, lanterns, and a 'folding cushion,' which looked like a miniature folding chair on which one could rest one's head without upsetting one's topknot.

Most interesting in the exhibition I found the two examples of so-called *dōchū-ki*, or 'guides for on the road.' One was the *Tōkaidō dōchū-ki*, a pocket-sized work with detailed maps and lengthy texts with colorful descriptions of famous landmarks. The other work on display was the *Kisōrō meisho ezu*, or *Pictorial Guide to the Famous Places along the Kiso Road*. They were packed with all kinds of practical information about life on the road: the distances from post station to post station, the prices of lodgings, the food on offer—even the names of the post station managers, or *tonya*, could be had.

A common theme running through guides like these was the need for travelers to act with restraint—a pretty sound reasoning given the Namamugi incident. There were plenty of dangers lurking on the road for the Edo period traveler. The inns along the road offered little when it came to privacy and hygiene; the average traveler had to share rooms with total strangers and often had to sleep in lice-infested bedding, and food poisoning was a frequent occurrence.

The temptations of prostitutes, who plied their trade from such inns, presented an additional threat, all the more treacherous as it came in the guise of pleasure. Recognizing this clear and present danger, the *Ryokō yōjinshū*, concluded:

It is wise to restrain your sexual desires when traveling, as most inn harlots carry a venereal disease. One should be extra careful during the hot summer months, when infections spread more readily. One might even catch something from the bedding, though this can be prevented by putting some repellent fragrance among your sleep-ware.

Apart from giving you something, people might also be out to get something from you. Unlike modern-day Japan where, up till recently, you could drop your wallet at the meeting point in Tokyo station and it would still be there when you returned, theft in Edo-period Japan was a constant menace, and one constantly had to look out for pickpockets.

In the more remote regions, there was the threat of highway robbers and, in forested areas, even bears. During rainy seasons, there was the threat of landslides and flooded rivers. But even in summer, there were sections where one had to travel by boat—a dangerous proposition for those who couldn't swim. Hence the common advice: 'Do not take a boat to shorten your trip.'

Yet despite all the lurking dangers, curiosity being what it is, people still wanted to travel. The guides not only catered to, but also fed this growing tourist industry. Next to the wood prints of Hiroshige and others, they became an advertising medium for the inns and other places along the route that served to keep the Edo traveler comfortable and happy. And though the Bakufu authorities did not encourage travel, neither did they forbid it.

Travel for leasure, in Japan, seriously took off during the first decades of the eighteenth century, a time of political stability and economic prosperity. Thousands of Japanese citizens began to hit the road, not just to look up relatives in other parts of the country, but also to visit a place of pilgrimage, a famous hot spring, or simply get some life experience. Thus the old proverb went: *kawaii ko ni wa, tabi ni saseyo* (send your beloved child on a journey).

Such journeys could last up to several months, especially in cases when one wanted to travel the length of the country.

The experiences on the road, in turn, spawned a whole new genre of travel literature, either in the form of *tabi nikki* (travel diaries), or *kikō bungaku* (travel literature).

One of the most successful examples of *dōchū-ki* was Jippensha Ikku's *Tōkaidōchū hizakurige* (*Shank's Pony along the Tōkaidō*), a picaresque novel about the misadventures of two mischievous Edoites on their travel along Japan's major highroad. When the first volume of Ikku's novel appeared in Edo's bookshops in 1802, it became an instant bestseller. Aware he had hit a profitable vein, Ikku kept writing, taking his characters from one side of the country to the other. By the time the last installment appeared in 1822, he had written twenty-one volumes.

Ikku taught his readers that traveling along Japan's major highroads wasn't always the solemn affair it was made out to be. That even the warrior class could (at least on paper) be made fun of is made clear at the outset of his story when, leaving a teahouse near Shinagawa, Ikku's heroes Kitahachi and Yajirōbei encounter the retinue of a *daimyō*:

The two frontmen were an old geezer in his sixties and a young chap of fourteen or fifteen. Both of them were simply servants from local inns.

FRONTMAN: Get down! Get down! Off with the headgear!

KITAHACHI: It seems elopers don't have to prostrate themselves.

YAJIRŌBEI: How come?

KITAHACHI: They already have their ears cut off, so they can hear just fine.

FRONTMAN: Packhorse driver! You just hold that horse's mouth!

KITAHACHI: How on earth is he going to shut up a horse? Hehehe.

FRONTMAN: You at the back there! Get down lower!

YAJIRŌBEI : Is he talking to me? I guess I'm too tall. After all, don't they call me the older brother of the Nine-Tattoo Dragon of Mount Atago?

Shortly after, they are (like our *samurai* friend at the Amazake Chaya) approached by a packhorse driver:

DRIVER: Gentlemen! This horse is on its way back. Won't you catch a ride?

YAJIRŌBEI : We'll get on if it's cheap.

DRIVER: You can ride for no more than drinking money. How bout two hundred pieces?

Having settled on a price, they pursued their journey from their elevated positions, the one behind the other, the bells of their horses going ching, ching, ching, while the horses whinnied when, approaching from the other direction, another packhorse driver called out, 'You bastard! You beat me to it!'

'Go and eat shit!' replied the former.

'Kiss my arse!' said the latter.

It seemed this kind of conversation was the regular mode of salutation among highroad packhorse drivers, as if they were bound by some solemn duty to hurl insults at each other whenever they passed.

Not only Ikku's writing was full of mischief. It is said that when he lay on his deathbed, he handed his friends small parcels, solemnly asking them to place them on his funeral pyre at his cremation. Assuming them to contained incense, they dutifully executed his dying wish, only to find to their consternation that the parcels contained firecrackers—even in death Ikku couldn't resist cracking a joke.

Hamamatsu

Having dropped off my gear at the BASE Outdoor Hostel in uptown Hamamatsu, I took the overhead railway down town. I was in the mood for *karee raisu* (curry rice), but it took me ages to find a place that served this common Japanese take on that great Indian invention.

As I wandered through Hamamatsu's downtown area, a group of young men crossed the street and somehow caught my attention. They were all immaculately dressed, their hair carefully manicured, and on their feet designer shoes. They strode along leisurely but confidently, not in the slavish shuffle of the *sarariman*. The tallest among them, upfront, his light blue silk jacket unbuttoned and his necktie removed, was approached by one of the many cute girls posted outside the restaurants to lure in customers. He didn't slow his purposeful pace—the rest followed suit—but kept looking forward as he faintly tilted his head sideways to dismiss her with the words: '*Mō kimatta!*' (We've decided!)'

A few blocks farther down I was about to cross the street when a white stretch limo pulled up to the curb. A man in uniform and white gloves leaped forward to pull open the doors while another one, who looked like a waiter, stood ready with a large bunch of flowers as the blue-lit interior released six giggling young women, all dressed for the night in tight-fitting skirts and elaborate coiffures.

One of them struggled to mount her stiletto heels and pull down her short skirt at the same time, exclaiming, '*Yada!*' (I hate it!), which caused the others, who had managed to pull it off more elegantly, to burst into yet more ebullient bursts of giggles.

How little had changed, I thought. A few centuries ago, the men would have crossed the street in wide-legged *hakama* and broad-shouldered *haori*, their two swords tucked into their *obi* below their navel and protruding from a pleat on their left hip, their hair in a perfect topknot. The women would have been dressed in the most beautifully embroidered *kimono* with *obi* to match, their elaborate coiffures ornamented with *kanzashi* and held together by long iron pins, and on their slender feet high-heeled *geta* as they emerged from their ornately lacquered palanquins.

Today the only physical reminder of that distant era was an, at least in its materials, faithful reconstruction of Hamamatsu castle. For almost two decades, between 1568 and 1586, the castle had been the home of Tokugawa Ieyasu, the warlord who completed the work begun by Oda Nobunaga and all but completed by Toyotomi Hideyoshi: to unite Japan under one ruler.

Ieyasu's career began precariously; more than once his life had hung on a silk thread, but he seems to have been born under a lucky star. His father, Matsudaira Hirotada was a minor chieftain and the master of Okazaki castle in the western part of the neighboring province of Mikawa. He was a vassal to Imagawa Yoshimoto, the powerful warlord from the neighboring province of Suruga. Ieyasu's mother was from the Mizuno clan. But when Ieyasu was three years old, they allied themselves with the Oda, the arch-enemy of the Imagawa, forcing his father to divorce his wife and send her back to her clan.

Three years later, Takechiyo, as Ieyasu was then still called, was sent to Sunpu as a hostage to Imagawa Yoshimoto. He never arrived. On his way there his escort was intercepted by Oda men. He was packed off to Atsuta, the 41st station along the Tōkaidō, and put under the guardianship of Katō Yorimori, a vassal to Oda Nobunaga, the young master of Nagoya castle, who controlled southern Owari. Yorimori's *yashiki* stood at a stone's throw from the ancient Atsuta shrine. It is believed that, during his stay at Atsuta, Takechiyo first encountered the eccentric Nobunaga. And it is said that the latter took a liking to the young Takechiyo, who was ten years his junior, and that he often took him along on his adventures.

For two years the life of the young boy hung in the balance, especially since his father refused to pay his son's ransom. Then, in 1549, Takechiyo's father was assassinated by one of his vassals. No longer of use to the Oda, the boy was swapped in a hostage exchange with the Imagawa. Though (given the death of his father) still a hostage, he effectively became a member of the Imagawa clan, receiving part of Yoshimoto's name (Motonobu) on his coming of age, and marrying the chieftain's niece. Nine years later, he fought his first battle, when he took part in the siege of Terabe castle, whose master had defected to the Oda.

Two years later Ieyasu's life again came close to reaching an untimely end when Yoshimoto was slain by Nobunaga in the Battle of Okehazama. Ieyasu, who had rode out into battle alongside his master, immediately withdrew his troops across the border into Mikawa. There he took refuge at the Daiju-*ji*, his ancestral temple near Okazaki castle. Retreating into the temple grounds, the seventeen-year old warrior prepared to commit suicide in front of his ancestor's grave, when the temple's chief priest implored him to reconsider: 'Does not the scripture teach us, "*Enriedo, gongujōdo?*" (Abhor this tainted world; Seek rebirth in the Pure World). Yet were you to pacify this tainted world while you are still in it, how much more would you enjoy the Buddha's divine protection!' And thus he installed himself in his clan's former castle of Okazaki, which had meanwhile been abandoned by the Imagawa following their lord's demise.

By the time Ieyasu had moved his headquarters from Okazaki to Hamamatsu, he was an influential chieftain, though much of it rested on his new alliance with his former enemy and one-time playmate, Oda Nobunaga.

Yet it was at Hamamatsu that Ieyasu suffered the greatest defeat in his long military career.

It was somewhere late in November 1572, that word reached Hamamatsu castle that Takeda Shingen had departed from Kōfu at the head of some twenty-five thousand troops and was marching down along the Tenryū River toward Hamamatsu. Ieyasu realized he was in grave danger. Shingen was a formidable foe. From his power base of Kai Province, he had steadily widened his sphere of influence to include large parts of surrounding provinces. He was so confident that, unlike most warlords, he didn't even have a castle, just a large mansion with a wide moat. This in accordance with his main motto: *Hito wa shiro; hito wa ishigaki; hito wa hori* (Men are castles; men are walls; men are moats)—in short, the shrewd warlord knew that it was all about human talent.

Any lingering doubts that Shingen was aiming for Hamamatsu were dispelled when, on 18 November, he laid siege to Futamata castle, some ten miles north of Hamamatsu and Ieyasu's first line of defense to the north.

Hearing of this, Nobunaga prudently advised his new ally to retreat to his former headquarters of Okazaki castle. But Ieyasu refused. 'I'd rather break my sword and become a monk than surrender all that I have gained at the first threat of danger.' Yet the odds were firmly against him. With a third of his men spread out over his growing territory, he was left with only eight thousand men. Tied down in his own battles, Nobunaga couldn't come to his aid either, though he did promise reinforcements.

For two anxious months, Ieyasu waited for Nobubaga's troops to arrive, all the while being harried by messengers from Futamata castle with requests for aid. But Ieyasu, aware he had too few men to come to their aid, wisely decided to stay put.

Finally, towards the middle of January, the reinforcements arrived. But delight turned to disappointment when Ieyasu realized they're only three thousand men strong. Even with their help, he would still be outnumbered by more than two to one. And they were too late. On January 22, 1573, having put up a stiff fight, their water supply cut off, his men at Furamata were forced to surrender.

Two days later, Ieyasu's scouts told him that Shingen was on the move again. He was following the Futamata highroad and heading straight for Hamamatsu. By the morning of January 25, his forces were within a few miles of the castle.

But then something strange happened. Having reached the hamlet of Kamijima, they suddenly turned and headed west, up the Hime Highroad towards Nagashino. Soon they had ascended Mikatagahara, an elevated plain just north of Hamamatsu. Ieyasu was stunned: could it be that Shingen was turning his back on him? It was the chance he had been hoping for. Though the plain was wide and flat, the road leading down the other side was steep and narrow: were he to attack Shingen in the rear there he would have him trapped.

Rallying his troops, Ieyasu hastily set out along the Honzaka Highroad, which intersected the Hime Highroad at the center of the plain. He reckoned that by the time he would catch up with his enemy, Shingen's troops would just be starting their descent on the plain's opposite side. But no sooner did he reach the plateau than his blood ran cold. There, facing him in full glory, was the combined force of Shingen's army in full battle array. Arranged in the impenetrable Fish Scale formation, their black banners boldly proclaimed the Takeda battle cry: *fūrinkazan* (swift as the wind; quiet as a forest; fierce as fire; immovable like a mountain).

Ieyasu had made the biggest blunder of his career, and he knew it. The wily fox had lured him from his castle and now had him trapped: there was no way Ieyasu could descend the plain without falling in the very same trap he had intended to set for his foe.

What followed was a crushing defeat by Shingen's famed cavalry. Overcome by grief over his terrible mistake, Ieyasu made ready to throw himself into the melee and fight to the death. But seeing this, one of his retainers grabbed the reigns of his horse and called out, 'Why sacrifice yourself? Let me fall in your place!' Saying this, he brought round Ieyasu's horse and struck its rump with the haft of his lance. Startled, the horse bolted, carrying Ieyasu back toward his castle.

Safely back at his castle, Ieyasu immediately ordered his men to leave the front gate wide open, light huge fires, and beat huge *taiko* drums to guide the remainder of his warriors back home. Seeing and hearing this, Shingen's scouts are said to have advised their lord not to attack the castle, fearing it might be a trap. Historians have pointed out that a similar episode is described in the Chinese classic *Romance of the Three Kingdoms*. And one wonders whether this popular tale, written during the 14th century, might not have been read by the erudite Ieyasu as a boy, inspiring him to use the same shrewd ploy as a grown man.

Interview

Ieyasu's story put me in mind of the two days I had spent in a London studio being interviewed for a documentary on the Japanese Warring States period.

Contrary to what I had expected, the studio was almost pitch dark. Instead of being bathed in bright light, the room had the air of a cave-like robber's den. Thick black cloth hung from the walls and had been draped over most of the equipment, while empty flight cases, stacked or just sitting around, littered the entire room. The only lighting was provided by a square box that emitted diffuse light onto a director's type chair at the center of the studio.

I was led to the dimly lit chair, where an assistant helped me rig up a microphone under my clothing. While he was busy, I was asked to peer into a small window that, by an ingenious contraption, made it look as if I was facing the interviewer, though, in reality, I was looking straight into the lens of the camera.

I had typed out my 'script,' fearful the discerning viewer might catch me out on some historical inaccuracy. And I had spent the weeks leading up to the interview rehearsing my lines, carefully crafted to find the right balance between historical accuracy and the need for dramatic detail.

As I prepared myself mentally, I could hear people behind the camera discussing something in whispers. It appeared to concern me, for I caught the director motioning at me, and not in a very happy way. Before long, the assistant director came up to me and asked, 'would you mind terribly if we would lend you a shirt?' I was wearing a long-sleeved cotton shirt with a low neck, just the kind of sporty feel I thought appropriate for the occasion. But apparently, my casual look did not conform with the image they wanted to project. If only I had listened to my girlfriend; she had asked me repeatedly, 'Shouldn't you be wearing a jacket?'

I felt my heart pounding as the man who had wired the microphone under my borrowed shirt gave his thumbs up to the sound man, who in turn asked me to speak a few sentences. All was right, and now the director, invisible from where I was sitting, instructed the two cameramen to start shooting—they were filming me from two angles, in portrait and silhouette. Then I saw the interviewer behind the window nod: we were ready to roll.

'OK William, could you please tell us how devastating his defeat at Mikatagahara was for Ieyasu?

I was chuffed: this was right up my alley. I had made a

careful study of the battle's aftermath and the repercussions it had on Ieyasu's alliance with that other great warlord, Oda Nobunaga. I looked straight into the camera in front of me and delivered my lines.

'Ieyasu's defeat at Mikatagahara was his closest-ever brush with death. In the end, he was only saved by the late hour at which the battle commenced and the valiance of his men—not his skill as a commander. Nobunaga, who had foreseen the outcome of such an uneven fight—both in sheer numbers and the experience of its commanders—commented on Ieyasu's defeat with the words: "*Furyō no ni teitaraku sōrō.*" That is: "His impudence has landed him quite a mess." Coming from Nobunaga, it was only a mild reproach.

'An average man might have wanted to forget about such an ignominious defeat—put it away, never to be mentioned again. Not so Ieyasu. He instead did a remarkable thing: he ordered an artist to Hamamatsu castle and had him paint his portrait. The result is far from flattering. Ieyasu, who is said to have vacated his bowels in the heat of battle, is clearly still rattled by his brush with fate—it is all there: the terror of facing death, the shame of defeat, the anguish of what lies ahead.

'It is said that much later, after he had pacified the country in the Battle of Sekigahara, and purveying his realm from his headquarters of Edo castle, Ieyasu still reserved a place in his quarters for this haunting painting, as if to remind himself of how close he had come by not heeding his own better instincts and the good counsel of his allies…'

I beamed with pride: I was sure I had nailed it—

'OK William, that was really great,' came the voice of the director from the dark. 'Now let's try that again and break it down a bit for the viewer. Just relax and describe the situation in your own words.'

I took a nervous swig from the bottled water they had strategically placed on an upturned flight case beside me. What was wrong with my account? And weren't these my own words to begin with? I was startled by the voice of the director telling the cameramen to roll again.

'OK, William, in your own words…'

I swallowed: there was nothing for it but to let go of my lines. I braced myself and took the leap.

'Being defeated at Mikatagahara was his…eh…Ieyasu's closest-ever brush with death. In the end, he was only saved by the late hour he and…eh…Shingen met in battle. Nobunaga anticipated the outcome and wrote to one of his…eh…generals, "*Furyō no ni teitaraku sōrō*." That is: "His impudence has landed him quite a mess."

'Now a…eh…normal man might have wanted to forget all about it, but not Ieyasu. He instead ordered a painter to Hamamatsu castle to…eh…do his portrait. The result is far from flattering. Ieyasu, who is said to have vacated his bowels at one point, is clearly still rattled by his…eh…brush with fate—it is all there: the terror of facing death, the shame of defeat, the anguish of what lies ahead.'

'OK William, that was great. Now let's just do it again,

maybe shorten it a bit, so the sentences run more smoothly, but in your own words, as you would to a friend…'

I took another nervous swig from the by now almost empty bottle and forced myself to face the camera again. By now I had completely lost my train of thought and began to blurt out random shards of text with little coherency.

'Mikatagahara was a total nightmare for Ieyasu, who was only saved by showing up late, though a normal man might have forgotten it altogether. Not Ieyasu. He instead ordered a painter to Hamamatsu castle. The result was far from flattering. He was so rattled by his brush that he vacated his bowels—it is all there: the terror, the shame, the anguish.'

'Well…eh…that was good William, but I think we need a bit more detail in there to help the viewer along. Just casually describe the situation as you believe it happened— in your own words, of course…'

After an hour of this back and forth my mouth felt like parchment, and despite the steady supply of water and the relative coolness of the studio, I began to break out into nervous sweat. The *visagiste*, who at first only occasionally leaned in to gently stroke down a protruding hair, started to come round ever more frequently, trying to airbrush away the obvious symptoms of stress with the aid of powders and brushes.

All the while the questions kept coming hard and fast: 'What was Shingen's plan?' 'Why was he similar to Nobunaga?' 'How was he different?' 'Why was Ieyasu angry at Nobunaga?' 'Why was Nobunaga angry at Ieyasu?' 'Why was the rotation of Shingen's cavalry so critical?' 'Did they overrun the gunners?' 'What happened at Shingen's camp?'—on and on it went.

Before long it felt as if, peering through his bomb shelter prism, the interviewer was hurling small incendiary devices at me in the form of questions; then waiting with glee for me to explode—or rather implode—on-screen.

Of course I had only myself to blame. Well in advance, they had sent me a long list of topics to choose from. And I, in my unbridled enthusiasm, had ticked off more than half—I had bitten off more than I could chew and was now thoroughly chocking on it.

Some of the questions threw me completely: 'Could you tell us something about Takeeda Shinjin's habit of boiling people alive?'

'?!?' I knew Takeda Shingen hadn't been the most kind-hearted of warlords, but boiling people alive?

For a moment I contemplated giving them what they wanted: 'Of course, it's a well-established historical fact that he spent many a leisurely hour cooking people in big cauldrons—he preferred them well-done, actually, with a sprinkling of salt and pepper.' But then the historian in me revolted. Did they know the fearsome Shingen was actually gay? That he had a long romantic involvement with the youth Kasuga Toratsuna, whom he had crowned one of his Four 'Heavenly' Kings, and the man credited with dictating the medieval bestseller on military strategy, the *Kōyō gunkan?* Shingen was so besotted with the dashing youth that he even drafted an oath promising to refrain from seeing or sleeping with anyone else but him.

Homosexual relations were far from uncommon in medieval Japan. In fact, it had a history that went all the way back to the early days of the Heian period, when women were barred from military and religious centers. The absence of female company gave rise to a practice called *wakashudō,* or *nyakudō,* which typically involved an older and a younger man. The practice was further stimulated (if that's the right word) by the master-apprentice system, by which a craft or art was traditionally passed on. Formally, a senior and experienced monk or warrior was expected to initiate a young novice in Buddhist practice or the martial arts. But behind the sliding doors, within the privacy of a monk's private quarters or a warrior's mansion, these relationships often took on an amorous nature. Supposedly, the initiative for this 'blossoming' was expected to come from the novice, but it seems more likely that—where this was the case—it was either done in response to intimidation or to advance one's clerical or military career. The term '*watakushi mo*' (#me too) hadn't been coined yet, and even if it had, it would probably have been construed the wrong way round. With time the practice became openly accepted, and warriors of standing like Shingen would ride out into battle with a retine of their favorite pages in tow.

Oda Nobubaga, too, was somewhat of an aficionado of this particular warrior pastime. Many know about the sticky end to which he came when he was assailed while spending the night at Kyoto's Honnō temple. Fewer know he was in fact rudely disturbed from his dalliances with his seventeen-year-old page, Ranmaru. Hence, many of the contemporary wood prints depict the two facing their assailants in just a *kosode*, though they might well have been stark-naked. Needless to say, this is discreetly glossed over by most history books, be they Japanese or English.

By the time we were done, late on Saturday afternoon, the tension in the studio was palpable It had been a long week and the crew had spent each day, from early morning till late in the evening, tuning their equipment, grooming their guests and getting their insights on tape. They hadn't banked on spending the last two days having to coach, coax, and cajole this bloody, poorly-dressed Dutchman through an endless repetition of ill-conceived lines that somehow didn't cut the grade.

I couldn't help seeing the irony of my predicament—my own Mikatagahara. Though on an infinitely smaller scale, I too had been rattled by my experience. I did not doubt my little death struggle was there for all to see—the terror, the shame, the anguish—though I took some pride in not having vacated my bowels in the heat of battle.

Chiryū

I had made up my mind to skip the stretch to Nagoya and pick up the trail again at Kameyama, on the other side of Ise Bay. I had lived in Chiryū for four years and I knew what I would find. Nagoya and its environs were no different from most other metropolises in Japan, and my time there had been more than enough to explore every last morsel of beauty in the region.

Chiryū had been the highroad's thirty-ninth post station and the headquarters of the factory where I had worked stood right along the short stretch of the road that had been lovingly preserved, lined with a dozen withered pine trees said to date back to feudal times.

At the back of our offices had been a small pantry where we were allowed to make and drink our instant coffee. It had just one small aluminum-framed window. I had often stood at that tiny window, wanting to get out and set off along the Tōkaidō and just keep on walking—simply walk until I had forgotten all about the endless flow of technical reports and machine software updates.

Working at Fuji hadn't been too bad, really: the pay was good, people were nice, and I was even allowed to show up in my casual clothing, not the grey Fuji uniform my Japanese colleagues were required to wear. Yet I still hated it: the fixed hours, the drab canteen food, the monotony of the endless string of technical reports and minute reiterations of existing manuals.

I felt no urge to visit it again. I knew all my foreign colleagues from then had long since left, finding employment closer to home after their stints in Japan. My Japanese colleagues might still be there, swatting away behind their tiny desks, but they were unlikely to remember me. The average turnover rate for translators at Fuji was three years. Our team was comprised of five translators so, given that twenty years had passed, they would have gone through some thirty-five foreign translators. Moreover, just like Westerners find it difficult to distinguish between Asians, the Japanese have considerable difficulty telling Westerners apart, even if they have far greater variety in skin-, hair-, and eye color. So it was even possible they would mistake me for someone else, though I thought the prospect funny.

Ama

I would be taking the ferry from Cape Anago to Toba on the Ise peninsula. As I boarded the bus at the main terminal at Toyohashi station, the young man from the office from where I had just purchased my combined bus and ferry ticket (which is considerably cheaper) was helping the driver to install the cash tray into the elaborate ticket machine mounted on most of Japan's busses. Apparently, there was a problem, for he had brought along a big screwdriver with which he was trying to pry the tray into the slot into which it should fit. It wouldn't. As the clock ticked away and the departure time drew near, the wriggling and prying grew increasingly frantic until, when the second hand hit the hour of our departure, I thought he was ready to plunge the tool deep into his abdomen in atonement for bringing such irreparable disgrace on his company. He was luckily preempted by the older bus driver, who leaned into his microphone and spoke the liberating words, 'Honored guests, it seems we have a slight technical glitch. Please bear with us for a few minutes until we have resolved the problem.' Put at ease, the attendant finally found the right angle, and with a last rattle, the obstinate tray snapped into position.

The bus driver had the air of a flight steward over him. Prior to our departure, he walked the length of the aisle, checking on passengers to make sure they were comfortable and answering questions from insecure old ladies. He also made sure I had a seat on the right-hand side of the bus: 'That way you'll have a better view of the sea.'

The customer service didn't stop there. Once we had departed he gave a running commentary on the bus's movement so as to forewarn his precious cargo: 'OK, here we go, I'm pulling up now…turning slightly to the left now…just waiting for the traffic lights here…here we go again…now a sharp turn to the right…' It was a refreshing change from the disinterested rudeness of Dutch bus drivers.

One of Ise's attractions is its female pearl divers. The pearls that are nowadays on the market are all cultivated, but up until the sixties of the previous century natural pearls were still being harvested by the so-called *ama*, or 'sea women,' who have been diving up oysters from the sea bed for thousands of years—sometimes at depths up to five fathoms.

The last time I was in Ise I had skipped the pearl fishers to go and see the Ise shrine. Well, not see it really. The shrine itself is only open to the public once a year. Worse still, they

were just getting ready for its twenty-year-cycle reconstruction, and I had to make do with a glimpse of its roof over
a building site fencing.

This time I had set my mind on seeing the *ama*. As late
as the nineteen fifties, some seventeen thousand *ama* were
still active around Japan's coast, filling the air with their
faintly haunting whistle so as to control the release of air
when they surface. They were considered to be superior to
male divers because of the distribution of their fat and their
remarkable ability to hold up air. By then most of them were
using wetsuits, though some still wore the white *amagi*,
which covers the whole body and is believed to scare off
sharks. Originally *ama* wore just a loincloth, but all that
changed when Westerners arrived and the Japanese had to
watch how Western women entered the sea fully dressed.

There are still some two thousand *ama* active in Japan.
And recently the world's female divers have been organizing
themselves in an effort to have themselves listed as an
Intangible Cultural Treasure. To achieve this the UNESCO
requires the Japanese *ama* to be accepted on Japan's own List
of Intangible Cultural Folk Properties. As a preliminary to
this, they have meanwhile been accepted as such by the local
prefecture of Mie.

Nowadays the traditionally clad *ama* no longer dive com-
mercially, but merely as a tourist attraction and to keep the
practice alive. To see them in action one has to visit
Mikimoto Island, which is situated in the port of Toba, and

is named after, Mikimoto Kōkichi, the man who first developed the art of cultivating pearls. Today the island can be reached by a walking bridge from the mainland. Roughly every hour the *ama* arrive in front of a raised visitor's platform, and spend the next fifteen minutes diving up oysters from the sea bed for a packed audience of tourists.

Afterward, I sat down behind the conveyor belt of a *kaiten sushi*, a cheap way to eat one's fill in *sushi* without having to empty one's wallet. One by one I lifted my favorites from the conveyor belt: salmon, *gunkan maguro*, *anago*, etc. The choices that weren't making the rounds were advertised by little signs with photos placed on saucers with the corresponding color-code indicating its price: expensive items like *toro* and *uni* in red, or a cheap bowl of hot clam soup in green. Then my jaw dropped: cheese salmon, cheese tuna, and then—as if they had no shame—cheese hamburgers, cheese fried potatoes, French fries, roast beef, chicken nuggets, and to top it all off, cheesecake and *tiramisu*. What!?! I understood that the march of civilization was unstoppable, but couldn't it for once please march past a *sushi* restaurant?

Video

It was Friday evening and I found myself alone in the lounge of the company dorm. All the guys had gone out drinking; I had a fencing contest the next day and wanted to stay sharp. There was no food. From Sunday till Thursday the kitchen was open, but not on Fridays and Saturdays: on those days you were expected to fend for yourselves. And so I made myself some *rāmen* and sat down in the lounge and switched on the TV to watch some CNN.

Bored by CNN's repetitive fare, my eyes fell on a bag of videos sitting next to the lounge's high-tech video system. The videos inside had no covers, just numbers; it was the way the video store worked: the empty covers were on the shelves for customers to peruse. Picking your choice, you would hand the covers in at the counter, where they would hand you the corresponding video.

Even without knowing the numbering code, I suspected what was on them. All the 'public' videos were in the cabinet under the huge TV screen; the ones in the bag were videos my dorm mates had viewed in their rooms. They could only be one thing: why watch them on tiny screens if you could watch them on the lounge's huge screen with surround sound to boot. They had left them there to be returned to the store over the weekend along with the ones from the lounge.

Me being me, I was curious, and so I slid the top one into the system's video player, pressed play, and sat back in one of the wide chairs as I slurped down my noodles.

I chuckled to myself. I had been more than right in my suspicions. The title, spread across the screen in pink lettering, spoke for itself: *Jigoku no fujin* (Housewives from Hell). After a few short scenes of atrocious acting, a dozen or so 'housewives' dressed in flimsy aprons quickly came to the point with a few *yakuza*-like blokes, their muscular bodies covered in tattoos. I fast-forwarded the video, and what followed was a string of increasingly graphic sex acts in every obscene combination and position one could—

There was a short clank of the lounge's metal door. There stood David Moseley, my English colleague from Fuji's translation department. In two years he had never once bothered to show his face, only to decide to come and pay me a visit on this particular evening at this particular hour. He stood there as nailed to the floor, staring at the writhing mass of flesh on the huge video screen, then at me eating my noodles, then back at the screen, as groans of carnal delight emanated from the surround-sound system.

It wasn't that Dave was a prig. Once, during lunch in the company canteen, he bent over toward the rest of us in a conspiratorial manner and related with relish how, the day before, his Japanese wife had pulled up at a traffic light on her bike and, looking sideways into the cabin of a nearby car, spotted a man having sex with a miniature sex doll. David was almost driveling by the time he had completed his story. No, it was more the shock of seeing your formal colleague engaged in something you would *never ever* want others to find out about yourself.

When I walked into the office on Monday morning I knew my reputation was in shatters. Dave was leaning over his desk towards the others in his conspiratorial manner again, clearly relating in equally salacious detail what he had witnessed the previous night.

It wasn't long before I was secretly whispered about in the company's corridors—albeit with reverence by some— as the guy who consumed porn over dinner in the company's dormitory lounge.

Cats

The Chōonzan Taikō temple in Mat*sushi*ta, just a few miles west of Toba, was and would be the most beautiful stay of my trip, hands down. I could say this with some certainty, as I already knew the places I would be visiting down the road. I had stayed here on my disastrous journey around the Ise Penninsula with my neighbor, Evert, and had almost forgotten its charm, despite the somewhat poor state of repair of its lodgings. I just loved the alcoved rooms, the enclosed garden, the pergola groaning under the weight of a sprawling wisteria, even the stern old lady who ran the place with an iron fist. When I told her I had stayed here before some years ago, she said I might be shocked at the change in price. But I told her she needn't worry, as I had no recollection of the price. Back then the place still advertised itself as a youth hostel, but more recently they had decided to raise the stakes and make it a proper *shukubō*, or priest's quarters, which also serve as lodging for pilgrims.

At the front of the temple, I got chatting with one of the priests who manned the small visitor's booth. Did I know this was a *shinbutsu shūgō* temple? I said I didn't have a clue, meanwhile trying to fend off the mosquitos who were already out in force.

'Let's go inside,' he said, 'and I'll make us some tea.' At this, he emerged from the booth and led me to an almost equally modest structure, but with a small table filled with memorabilia and tea-making equipment.

'Yes, it means syncretism of *kami* and Buddhas,' he began as he punched hot water into a teapot from a vacuum thermos bottle. 'When Buddhism first arrived in Japan during the sixth century, it was adopted by the native Shintō religion. Temples became attached to shrines; shrines became attached to temples. Thus our temple has a long and deep affiliation with the shrines of Ise and nearby Futami Okitama. They never really fused but became deeply linked. It remained like that right up until the Meiji period when the government separated the two.

'It wasn't that they rejected Buddhism, they just wanted to insulate Shintō so they could use it for their own political purposes. Yet it triggered a fierce anti-Buddhist movement among the people. Thousands and thousands of temples throughout the country were demolished, their lands seized, and monks were forced to become Shintō priests or return to being laymen. Luckily our temple was spared, though the Okitama shrine that used to be situated on the temple grounds was forcibly relocated to Futami-ura, which is why it is now called the Futami Okitama shrine.'

'Why was there so much hostility toward the Buddhist church?' I queried as I slurped from my hot tea.

'You must know that, in the seventeenth century, each household had been forced to become affiliated to a local temple. It's called the *danka* system. The measure was partly meant to stamp out Christianity, which was seen as a threat to the state—people had to prove they weren't Christian by attaching themselves to a temple. But the contributions they had to pay were often more than they could bear.'

'Aren't most Japanese households still attached to a local temple?' I asked.

'Yes, but today it's no longer compulsory.'

I remarked on the large number of cats prowling about the temple

'Yes, it's always been like that. In fact, we once had a cat who guided visitors up the long flight of stairs leading up to the temple. They even came over from America to film a documentary for Animal Planet. There was a massive increase in the number of visitors after that. And even now, whenever they rescreen it, we have a fresh wave of visitors.'

I said I loved cats.

'Then you've come to the right place. Recently we've founded the Aiju monastery for pets, which celebrates the close bond between humans and animals.'

Sterling Performance

Partly by way of a lark, and partly—well, mostly really—as a justified revenge for his eagerness to spread the word on my nocturnal misdemeanors, I decided to pull a trick on David. He happened to have a somewhat smug but lovable habit of expressing how content he was with his linguistic acumen by declaiming, 'Sterling performance Moseley!' whenever he had completed a translation and hit the 'save' command. My revenge was a simple operating system extension I had downloaded that allowed you to allocate various sounds to specific commands.

I was still making my own music and I had just bought myself a Korg synthesizer and a Lexicon reverb. The Korg had some terrific samples, including one of a cheering football stadium, while the Lexicon had spatial reverbs that just blew your mind. Working away in my desktop studio over the next weekend, I composed a short sound bite that, with the help of my dodgy extension, would put David in his place: it opened with the kind of trumpet volley played when medieval kings held court, set against a stadium's crescendoing applause and ending with the deeply reverberating laudation: 'Sterling performance Moseley-ley-ley!'

Testing it on my computer I tweaked the extension until it played the soundbite whenever one pressed the 'save' command. You could adjust the volume, and though It was a pretty unstable piece of software, it managed to do the trick most of the time. I was chuffed with myself for hitting just the right tone: a measured rebuke to David's habitual self-appraisals, and a nice diversion for our small but tightly knit group of translators. After all, even though the office floor was huge, only we would be able to hear it, and all of us— even Dave—would appreciate the joke. I couldn't wait to see it all in action.

I stayed on late that Monday until all the other guys from my team had left. Scanning the floor for suspicious eyes, I sat down behind David's computer, installed the extension and sound bite into his operating system, and rebooted. After an anxious minute, the usual desktop image appeared: the computer still seemed to work fine. I set the extension's volume to its minimum and hit the 'save' command. It worked! Though less impressive than on my stereo studio speakers, the computer's small speaker still managed to convey the spatial feel of the original. I spent another few minutes tweaking the volume, loud enough so we could hear it, quiet enough so as not to reach beyond our circle.

The next morning I acted as normal and greeted David with the usual 'Hi mate,' as he sat down behind his desk, spun round in his seat, hit his computer's power button, and began to work through his emails. This usually took him half an hour. More than an hour passed and there was still no sound from his computer; I seriously began to wonder if the extension was working as I had—

'TATARA-TATA-TAAAA… STERLING PERFORM-ANCE MOSELEY-LEY-LEY-LEY!!' Dave veered back in his seat in terror. For some inexplicable reason, the volume settings I had tweaked so carefully the previous evening had been lost. Instead, a heavily distorted soundbite now blasted forth from his computer at full throttle, the small speaker groaning under the weight of the studio-level dynamic range. Switching to damage-control mode, David tried to shut down all his open applications, but these actions too seemed to trigger the extension to do its dastardly work— clearly, the software was a shoddy piece of work: 'TATARA-TATA-TAAAA…STERLING PERFORMANCE MOSELEY -LEY-LEY-LEY!! TATARA-TATA-TAAAA…STERLING PERFORMANCE MOSELEY- LEY-LEY-LEY!!'

Too embarrassed to admit I had been behind this unheard-of breach of Japanese office etiquette, I acted as if nothing had happened, peering at my screen intently as if I were working on some particularly difficult translation.

My behavior was quite at odds with the rest of the office. Around us, our Japanese colleagues were beginning to look both angry and embarrassed, while farther away people began to stand up behind their desks to see what on earth had disturbed the disciplined murmur that otherwise reigned throughout the office.

David by now had his red head flat on his desk in a feeble attempt not to be associated with his screaming computer. It didn't help. Some ten desks away, Furuuchi-*san*, our humorless manager, had also stood up. Sadly, he too failed to see the funny side of it. Meanwhile, the bogus extension had gone totally haywire, randomly generating fresh laudatory messages without finishing the previous one: 'STERLING PERF—STE'STE'STE, PE'PE, MOSELEY-LEY-LEY-LEY!!'

Then all fell silent. On the other side of Moseley's desk stood a fuming Furuuchi-*san*, in his trembling hand the disconnected power cord to David's computer.

Yagyū Kaidō

Having rejoined the Tōkaidō at Kameyama, I was passing through the beautifully preserved post town of Seki, when I had an epiphany, or rather a change of heart. The weather would be turning foul in a few days and I was running out of time. Yet I desperately wanted to walk the Yagyū Kaidō, the old path that connected the ancient temple town of Nara with Kasagi village, on the Kizu River. I had more than a passing interest in this area. For some ten years, I had been researching and writing the history of the famed Yagyū, a local clan of *samurai* warriors whose village lay a few miles south of Kasagi and who had lent their name to the ancient highroad. They had founded the Yagyū Shinkage-ryū, a school of swordsmanship still practiced in Japan today.

And so I decided to skip the last leg of the Tōkaidō and instead jumped on the local train to Nara. From there I could follow the Yagyū Kaidō all the way to Kasagi, from where I could make my way back to Kyoto. I had no qualms about straying from the official route. I had just made a wide detour through Ise, and on my walk along the Nakasendō, too, I had made a detour through Kōfu to see Mount Fuji.

The first section of the Yagyū Kaidō is the most beautiful. The path starts out at Nara's Kasuga shrine, where it enters the trees and, twisting and turning through primeval forest around a small brook, gradually ascends towards the Tōge no Chaya, the Tea House at the Pass. From there it gradually descends to the Yabashira shrine, some three miles west of Nara.

Just how treacherous this path can be was on clear display at one section, which was all but covered in uprooted trees and other flotsam from some recent typhoon. Only the huge ancient flagstones had remained unmoved by the forces of nature, as they would for ages to come.

Along the path, on exposed rock faces higher up, were age-old engravings of *jizō*, the Ksitigarbha Bodhisatva, the Earth Bearer, who guards over all those who dwell in the six worlds between the death of Buddha and the return of his successor, Maitreya. Given that *jizō* are especially considered the protector of children and travelers, it is not surprising that so many can be found among this most beautiful, but equally most dangerous stretch of the Yagyū Kaidō.

Just before I reached the Kōzan shrine, at a cross-section with the most beautiful toilet building I've ever seen, was a statue with a kind of red apron draped around its neck. A man who was having a drink from his thermos bottle at the nearby rest place came up to me and pointed out the skirt was meant to hide the shameful conduct of a *samurai* who had once tested his sword by cutting off the statue's head. And indeed, as I looked more closely, I could see the head had been separated from the statue's trunk with a clear cut.

Wow! This swordsman really had issues. To cut a random rock in two, fine—but to cut off the head of a religious statue? A nearby sign read:

This is the *Kubikiri Jizō* [Cutthroat Jizō] of which it is said that Araki Matauemon used it to test his sword. Judging by the carving technique, the statue is believed to date back to the Kamakura period.

A native of the village of Araki, only ten miles west from Yagyū village, Matauemon had spent his youth in Yagyū village, studying the Yagyū Shinkage-ryū under the Yagyū brothers, Munenori and Mitsuyoshi.

I was glad this piece of vandalism was the work of just a student, and not any of the Yagyū swordsmen, or I would have had to revise my view of them drastically—though they might have taught their students not to cut off the head of a *jizō* that had stood there for centuries.

I reflected how, some seven hundred years ago, a small band of men including two Yagyū brothers must have passed the same statue in the company of none other than the emperor. They had accompanied the then Emperor Go-Daigo, who had been forced to flee from his palace in Kyoto after he had sought to wrest back power from the military Bakufu in Kamakura. Dressing himself up as a woman, he had initially fled to Nara's Tōdai temple, where he spent the night in heated talks with the temple's abbot, brainstorming where he could find a safe refuge. In the end, they had decided on Kasagi-*dera*, the ancient temple atop Mount Kasagi along the Kizu River.

To accompany his highness along the treacherous Yagyū Kaidō, they had chosen the Yagyū clansmen, one of whom, a warrior-monk by the name of Gensen, was connected to the temple.

Thus it was that, on a late Sunday evening, September 29, 1331, a small group of men escorted the imperial palanquin. All in all, there were some two dozen men. Apart from Gensen and his warrior-brother, Nagayoshi, there were a handful of monks who had joined the entourage at the Tōdai temple. Then there were the nobles who had fled the court along with the emperor: the Great Counselor, Kintoshi, the Middle Counselor, Madenokōji Fujifusa, and the Rokujo Lesser Marshal, Minamoto no Tadaaki—all dressed in plain clothing.

Guided by the Yagyū brothers, they had safely reached Mount Kasagi and its temple. There, with the help of the powerful local warlord Kusunoki Masashige, they had valiantly fought off Bakufu forces. For a month they managed to hold out atop the mountain. But on the night of October 30, a small band of enemy warriors managed to scale the mountain's eastern slope and set fire to the temple. Only a handful of monks and the two Yagyū brothers had survived, though the latter were stripped of their lands. Go-Daigo was sent into exile to Oki island, in the Sea of Japan.

For a while, it had seemed that with Go-Daigo's exile the Yagyū were doomed to follow the fate of so many other small clans during Japan's almost three centuries of civil war. Countless were the times they came to total annihilation. Then, just at their darkest moment, having in short succession lost their independence, their castle and their lands, their fortune changed almost overnight when, in 1594, one of their members, the hugely talented Yagyū Munenori, was invited to give a demonstration of his clan's art of fencing for none other than Tokugawa Ieyasu.

Ieyasu had been encamped at Takagamine, on the banks of the Kamo River, just north of Kyoto. Like dozens of other warlords, he had been required to contribute laborers for the large-scale reconstruction of Fujimi castle. The then ruler, Toyotomi Hideyoshi, had chosen the site to receive an embassy from China in order to sign a truce following his disastrous Korean invasions. Ieyasu was more than impressed with the Yagyū swordsman—who beat him hands down in a friendly duel—and hired him as his private fencing instructor. It was with Ieyasu's rise to Shōgun, a decade later, that Munenori was promoted to the rank of *daimyō* and that his clan's future was secured.

A little higher up the old highroad, I spotted a deer among the trees. It balked when I approached. Apparently, it had grown tired of all the noisy Chinese tourists in Nara and wandered off to seek some quietude in the forest.

I was glad to reach the halfway teahouse around noon. I hadn't had anything to eat that morning, not even coffee, even though I had got up especially late for Japanese standards—nine o'clock—but every place I passed had been closed. It seemed tourism had made Nara's entrepreneurs somewhat lazy.

Though its exterior was in tiptop shape, its interiors looked a bit worse for wear. There were a few baskets on shelves with crisps and a small glass vitrine with some canned drinks. An old man sat on the side of the raised floor with faded *tatami*, but waved his hand in front of his face when I asked if they served any *soba*.

He looked at me as if I spoke Uighur, but then he pointed at his mouth and complimented me on my Japanese.

I thanked him but expressed my disappointment, saying I had looked forward to some ice-cold *zarusoba*.

'*Iya*,' he said as he shook his head again, 'we're only open on Saturday and Sunday. But we don't do *soba* then either.'

So I decided to go for my fix of *aminosan-nado*, or 'monosodium glutamate, etc.' (the 'etc.' is the tricky bit), and bought myself a packet of Japanese crisps, praying my stomach would hang on in there.

Near the Enjō temple, I luckily found a small shop that served *kitsune udon* to fill my empty stomach and help dissolve some of the 'etc.' toxins.

I had almost reached Yagyū village when I saw on my map I could make a shortcut through the hills by following a hiking trail. That way I could save myself some precious time, as it was already late and I wanted to spend the night in Kyoto.

I should have known better. I had made similar errors of judgment on my trip along the Nakasendō two years earlier and it had cost me dearly.

To start with, I couldn't find the trail—a sure warning not to proceed any further. It was supposed to connect to a paved road that ran up to a small farm at the foot of the hills, but when I reached it, the road simply terminated in a rice paddy behind the farm. There was just no trace of any path up into the hills, and no kindly old lady in an apron to help me out like two years earlier.

And so, instead of doing the clever thing and turning back, I began to prod the dense forest edge in search of the path, though I first had to circumvent an electrified fence around a paddy. I eventually found something that vaguely resembled a path, but after only a few hundred yards it dissolved among the trees and undergrowth.

And so I began to ascend the slope, at first following a small and rocky stream, which petered out into a clearing in the undergrowth. This was good, but as I approached the summit, the slope grew steeper and steeper. At one point I could hardly find a foothold for my next step, but as soon as I paused, swarms of mosquitos descended on my exposed arms and legs, forcing me to plod on.

I eventually made it to the other side, where through sheer luck I stumbled back onto the official Yagyū hiking path.

It was already late when I finally reached Kasagi, but I just couldn't pass through it without having seen the temple and castle ruins atop Mount Kasagi. I was glad I did, for the giant frescoes on the mountain's eastern rock surfaces were stunning.

I thought I was the only tourist on the mountain, but as I made my way toward the stairs leading down to the village, I bumped into a young Japanese couple. They seemed just as surprised as me, for she gave a start and he also made a sound of surprise: '*hora!*'

Having negotiated the one-mile long flight of stairs down to the village in near-dark, I tried to find my way to the train station, when one of those small, box-shaped family vans pulled up beside me. It was the young couple. '*Sugoi naa!*' she exclaimed as she lowered the window. 'You're just as fast as us and we drove down by car.'

'Yes, but this route is much shorter,' I countered.

I asked them if they knew there still was a train bound for Kizu, where I could switch to a train to Kyoto.

'We don't know. We never take trains. But hop in and we'll drive you there.'

'All the way to Kizu?'

'Yes, why not,' he said cheerily.

'We have often been helped by others in the past,' she added, 'so it's a pleasure to help someone else instead.'

Their names were Yoko and Kyōsuke, and they both worked on a tea farm, though not the same one. He was originally from Osaka, she from Okazaki. When I said I had lived in nearby Chiryū she expressed her surprise: '*Eeee?*'

I told them I had come past a small tea plantation walking the length of the Yagyū Kaidō, which elicited yet more exclamations of surprise, so I thought I'd better spare them the news that I had started out from Tokyo for fear of Kyōsuke-*san* fainting at the wheel.

'There are many, many really small tea farms in this region,' Yoko-*san* explained as she turned around in her seat. 'I happen to work at a somewhat larger one, but even we have just twenty staff.'

I asked her how tea is made.

'There are a few basic methods for making tea. Oolong tea, of course, is partially fermented; regular Japanese tea is just made of dried tea leaves, while the leaves for the pounded *matcha* tea come from shaded bushes.'

By the time they dropped me off at Kizu station, it was

already getting on towards eight. I once again said how thankful I was at them having rescued me at this late hour, then made my way toward the escalator up to the platforms. I turned round to wave. They were still there, standing side by side, waving but otherwise perfectly still beside their car, like the ancient *jizō* statues along the Yagyū Kaidō.

Kiyomizu

By the time I checked in at my capsule hotel in Kyoto, the bad weather front had reached central Japan—it was now pouring down thick and fast. I was glad I had rearranged my itinerary to walk the Yagyu Kaidō. Had I been walking it now I might find myself battling upstream against a deluge of tree trunks and mud.

The next morning I walked the short stretch up from the hostel towards the Kiyomizu temple. Of all of Kyoto's temples, I find it somehow the most soothing.

Sitting on the western slope of Mount Otawa and supported by a dense structure of pillars without a single nail, the main building has survived for almost four centuries—not a small feat in a country frequently rocked by earthquakes. It was Tokugawa Iemitsu, who built the present temple in 1633, though the original temple was founded even earlier.

It is said that, somewhere toward the end of the eighth

century, Enchin, a Buddhist monk from the Hossō sect, climbed Mount Otowa in search of a mythical golden stream. Instead, he encountered an old man sitting on a log of wood, and who went by the name of Gyōei. He told the monk he had sat there for more than two hundred years, immersed in reverent prayer to the great Kannon, the Goddess of Mercy, who has postponed her enlightenment to stay behind and help those who suffer in this world. But now he wanted to go on a pilgrimage, and thus he asked Enchin to take his place. Gyōei never returned. But going in search of the old man, Enchin found his sandals on the mountain's summit—a clear sign he had met none other than Kannon himself. Inspired by his encounter, Enchin returned to the wooden log to sculpt it into the old man's image, but never really got close to truly capturing the deity's divine features. For the next twenty years, the monk daily ascended the mountain's slope to continue his labor of love, until the year 778, when he met the wealthy Heian general Sakanoue no Tamamuro, who was so taken by the monk's plight that he donated his Kyoto residence to provide shelter for the monk, and had it moved to the mountain's lower slope, that it might serve as a temple to this fleeting meeting between man and god.

As usual, the temple's wide terrace was groaning under the weight of tourists, mostly foreigners. Some of them had clearly already spent some time in Japan, judging by the way they were gobbledygooking in the *gaijin* stock phrases that sound like Japanese but mean nothing: '*Anno, soo desu nee, nanka, yappari…*' ('I was like, really, you know…')—ad infinitum, ad nauseam.

Kiyomizu means 'purifying water,' after a spring-fed waterfall that rushes under its mighty structure, but I felt no urge to cleanse myself: it had been a good trip, and I had thoroughly enjoyed large parts of it. Given how much of the old Tōkaidō ran through some of the most densely populated areas in the world, there was a lot of man-made ugliness too. One could even argue that the old highroad bore part of the blame in that it helped to hasten the spread of modernization.

All this, of course, was inevitable, as it is inevitable all around the world. Yet why did it have to be at the loss of so much heritage, so much good taste, so much beauty? Why did they have to systematically spoil their stunning coast, forcing Japanese holidaymakers to flee to Hawai and other overseas destinations to enjoy a bit of unspoiled beach, even though they have more than twenty thousand miles of coastline all to themselves? Why did they have to build *pachinko* parlors next to temples, factories in living areas, viaducts above national treasures?

At least in the last respect it seemed there was a glimmer of hope, though patience remains the operative word. Already in 2005, again under pressure of local citizen groups, the Koizumi government endorsed a plan to move the expressway over Nihonbashi bridge underground. It took twelve years for the Tokyo Metropolitan Government to 'begin a study' with the 'goal' of beginning construction 'after' the 2020 Tokyo Summer Olympics.

I would strongly advise against holding one's breath.

And why could the authorities not come up with such initiatives by themselves? After all, one doesn't have to look hard to realize there is plenty of material around to work with. The country is littered with similar or even worse examples.

In some ways it felt as if, rather than making progress, the authorities had regressed in their policies, abandoning concepts embraced centuries ago. Thus, where the Edo Bakufu had ordered the Tōkaidō to be lined with fragrant pine trees to offer shade and coolness; today's authorities relied on car-owners to turn on their air-conditioning over the sweltering tarmac, leaving under-age cyclists and old-age pedestrians to their simmering fate.

Still, I *had* succeeded in what I had set out to do: to find beauty along the Tōkaidō. I had found it at Kamakura, among the grounds of the Hachiman shrine and the Daibutsu. I had found it along the Hakone trail, with its rejuvenating *onsen* and its historic *amazake* tea house. I had found it at Seki, the last post town before one enters the Suzuka Mountains on the Tōkaidō's last leg to Kyoto. And I had found it in spades along the Yagyū Kaidō, though that didn't really count.

Most importantly, I had had plenty of meaningful encounters—at least as many as on my trip along the

Nakasendō. I found this reassuring: my fears that modernization had made people less open, less willing to interact with other human beings, had been unfounded. And that, in the end, was a most beautiful thing.

Glossary

ama:	Female pearl divers.
amagi:	White gown worn by ama while diving.
amazake:	Low-alcohol beverage made through a fermenting process using the *kōji* mold.
anago:	Conger eel.
bentō:	Lunch.
bessō:	Summer house.
chāshū:	Chinese-style marinated pork.
chaya:	Tea house.
daimyō:	Feudal lord.
danka:	Household supporting a Buddhist temple.
deshi:	Apprentice.
dōchū anzen:	Safe journey.
dōchū-ki:	Guide for on the road.
dōhan:	Paid date.
fugu:	Blowfish.
fujin:	Housewife.

furo:	Bath.
fusuma:	Sliding door.
gaijin:	Alien.
gannen:	First year of an era.
geba-geza:	Stand down and sit down.
genba:	Crime or building site.
geta:	Wooden clogs.
gunkan sushi:	Rice wrapped in *nori* and topped with crab salad or other soft topping.
hakama:	Trousered dress worn by *samurai*.
haori:	Silk jacket worn with a *hakama*.
hirune:	Siesta.
irimoya:	Gabled, hipped roof.
jigoku:	Hell.
jinrikisha:	Rickshaw.
jizō:	Guardian deity of children and travelers.
kachigumi:	Winners.
kaiten sushi:	Conveyor-belt *sushi* shop.
kami:	God(s), specifically Shintō deities.
kanzashi :	Ornaments used in traditional Japanese hairstyles.
karee raisu:	Curry rice.
kasu:	Residue of the *sake*-making process.
kasuzake:	Low-alcohol beverage made from fermented rice.
keibi-in:	Traffic guard.
kikō bungaku:	Travel literature.

kirisute gomen:	Authorization to cut and leave for dead.
kōji:	*Aspergillus oryzae,* a filamentous fungus (mold) used in Japan to ferment foodstuffs.
kosode:	Short-sleeved undergarment.
matcha:	Pounded green tea.
maguro:	Tuna.
makegumi:	Losers.
menma:	Pickled bamboo shoots.
michi:	Road.
miso:	Soup made of fermented bean paste.
mitsumata:	Oriental paper bush.
mizu:	Water.
mottainai:	Too good to be wasted.
narutomaki:	Fish cake.
nyakudō:	Homosexuality—typically between an older and a younger man.
nekkutai:	Necktie.
nenbutsu:	Buddha mindfulness practice.
nori:	Dried seaweed.
obi:	Sash or belt.
omoshiroi:	Interesting.
onsen:	Hot spring.
pachinko:	Pinball parlor.
rōnin:	Masterless samurai.
ryō:	Gold currency unit in pre-Meiji Japan.
ryōkan	Inn.
saka:	Slope.

sarariman:	Office worker.
sashimi:	Slices of raw fish.
sensei:	Teacher.
seppuku:	Ritual disembowelment.
shiatsu:	Acupressure.
shukubō:	Priest's quarters.
soba:	Buckwheat noodles.
tabi nikki:	Travel diary.
taikō:	Japanese percussion instrument.
tatami:	Straw mat.
tera:	Temple.
tempura:	Deep fried fish or vegetables.
tomometsuke:	Inspector accompanying a *daimyō*'s procession.
tonya:	Station manager.
toro:	Fatty meat from the belly of a tuna.
umami:	a category of taste corresponding to the flavor of glutamates.
uni:	Sea urchin.
wakashudō:	Homosexuality—typically between an older and a younger man.
waratabi:	Traditional straw sandals.
washi:	Japanese paper.
yakuza:	Homegrown Japanese maffia.
yashiki:	*Samurai* mansion.
yū:	Hot (spring) water.

TOYO REFERENCE SERIES
SAMURAI TRAILS
LUCIAN SWIFT KIRTLAND
EDITED BY WILLIAM DE LANGE

TOYO REFERENCE SERIES
TRAVELING JAPAN'S
DEEP INTERIOR
ISABELLA LUCY BIRD
EDITED BY WILLIAM DE LANGE

TOYO REFERENCE SERIES
CAPTIVE IN JAPAN

VASILY GOLOVNIN
EDITED BY WILLIAM DE LANGE

TOYO REFERENCE SERIES
HEARN'S JAPAN
VOLUME I
LAFCADIO HEARN
EDITED BY WILLIAM DE LANGE

TOYO REFERENCE SERIES
HEARN'S JAPAN
VOLUME 2
LAFCADIO HEARN
EDITED BY WILLIAM DE LANGE

TOYO PRess: Explore Dream Discover

Editorial supervision: Letitia van der Merwe. Book and cover design: Chōkei Studios. Printing and binding: IngramSpark. The typefaces used are Cardo and Prescript.